C000115379

Legacies

Prometheus
Orpheus
Socrates

Also by Joan M. Erikson

WISDOM AND THE SENSES

VITAL INVOLVEMENT IN OLD AGE
(with Erik H. Erikson and Helen Q. Kivnick)

ACTIVITY, RECOVERY, GROWTH
(with David and Joan Loveless)

SAINT FRANCIS AND HIS FOUR LADIES

THE UNIVERSAL BEAD

Legacies

Prometheus

Orpheus

Socrates

Joan M. Erikson

W. W. Norton & Company

New York   London

Copyright © 1993 by Joan M. Erikson
All rights reserved
Printed in the United States of America
First Edition

The text of this book is composed in 12 on 14 Bembo
with the display set in Centaur Bold and Bembo Italic
Composition by PennSet, Inc.
Manufacturing by Courier Companies

Library of Congress Cataloging-in-Publication Data
Erikson, Joan M. (Joan Mowat)
Legacies : Prometheus, Orpheus, Socrates
/ Joan M. Erikson.
p. cm.
Includes bibliographical references.
1. Prometheus (Greek mythology)   2. Orpheus
(Greek mythology)   3. Socrates.   I. Title.
BL820.P68E75   1993
292.1'3—dc20   92-37846

ISBN 0-393-03443-7

W. W. Norton & Company, Inc.
500 Fifth Avenue, New York, N.Y. 10110
W. W. Norton & Company Ltd.
10 Coptic Street, London WC1A 1PU

1 2 3 4 5 6 7 8 9 0

For William Alfred

Acknowledgments

I have used the pronoun "we" often in this book, as though it had actually been written by a team, and indeed so many have had a hand in the writing that "we" is truly appropriate.

I wish first to address my deep gratitude to William Alfred who has been my mentor for decades, spurring me on and giving me unstinting support in all my varied literary efforts. Without his support I would never have undertaken "Prometheus Unbound." I also wish to express my appreciation for the consistent encouragement and editorial help given me by Ilana Fortgang. The members of Inge Hoffmann's seminar, especially Inge herself, read and offered helpful ideas as the manuscript was in first draft. Kimberly Patton expertly caught errors in the noted "facts" of Orpheus' life—for which I am most grateful. Richards Beekman was extremely helpful in directing me to pertinent material on shamanism, presented in the Orpheus chapter. Michael Siegell directed me to the enriching and clarifying concept of *rasa* as understood and revered in India. The manuscript was read through and unclarities brought to my attention by Dorothy Austin when I was most in need of a reading and comment. Doone Williams provided a meticulous search for faulty grammar and muddy sentence structures as well as much discussion of the book's content. I am indebted to Katherine Holmes who was immensely helpful in reproducing all of the selected illustrations. Thanks also to Robert J. Gray for his delightful sketches of various ancient harps. I must also include two valiant supporters from a number of years ago who saw me through my earliest writing about Orpheus. Thank you Arden Parish and May Hipshman, you were true abettors and friends.

Finally, I would like to express my deepest appreciation to Lorraine Gray who skillfully helped to weave the manuscript through many versions. Her clarity of thought was a consistent and invaluable contribution.

And last but always, if ever man were muse—surely mine is Erik.

Contents

Legacies

Prometheus

Orpheus

Socrates

Prologue

We live, undeniably, in a technologically oriented world where science and certainty are in charge. But we are of course not actually robots in a mechanized world; our human heritage is animal, part instinctual, and we therefore often become overwhelmed, out of synchronicity with the dominant regime. Myths and legends, in their hoary timelessness, offer us release and play in an amazing world where things fall up and fly down naturally. This unworldly respite is refreshing and freeing, like daytime dreaming that "knits up the raveled sleeve of care," as Shakespeare phrased it.

But just what does the word "myth" mean? Where does it come from? Partridge's *Etymological Dictionary of Modern English* says that the word derives from the Greek *muthos*, speech, a narrative, and is related to Indo-European *mudh*, to imagine. As we follow the permutations, we come to Greek *muthologia*, discourse and logic, and finally we reach English *mythopoeic*, poetic, poem.[1] So here we have speech, narrative, imagination, logic, and poetry to include in a genealogy of the genre of myth.

Careful study of the myths and legends of the world reveals astonishingly little variation in plot. Everywhere human beings have been faced with the same problems. Our bodies are similar and the development of all *homo sapiens* follows a similar physical timing; our psyches are timed accordingly. What could be really new about the life cycle, considering the astoundingly universal nature of human experience, as people born out of entirely different environments nevertheless pass through processes of growing older which are remarkably alike? We are ultimately all of one species: *Homo sapiens, Homo ludens, Homo erectus,* of common origin—homogeneous—us—where planet earth is home. The one element in these myths that may surprise us is the originality of the mortal mythical characters: their multiple ways of facing and solving the universal problems of living, loving, hating, and dying, and the imaginative solutions created to cope with a longing for immortality. The immortal ones, too, have problems, but they have time to work things out.

Myths are the prehistory of humankind, so the scholars tell us. Told and retold in heroic legend and fairy tale by the "old ones," the shamans and the sages, they have been passed on to children, the child in all of us. Given visual reality by graphic artists, sung by music makers, and danced in dramatic, ritual celebration, they have remained vital through the centuries. The graphic arts crystallize myth's form, which may live on without further development or may finally evolve into decorative styles. But whereas the work of graphic artists and sculptors has been remarkably preserved against time and is our legacy, dance and music have, to our loss, not been recorded until more recent times.

When the writing of words was invented, the "old ones" worried that recording would usurp the discipline of memory and weaken inner commitment to the content, to the felt meaning of the intended teaching. This concern was justified. To learn by heart and repeat from memory gives poetry and song a dimension of inner authority that is seldom possible in the reading. With the tool of writing, however, new myths began to be exchanged among various literate cultures. Dramatic artists celebrated chosen heroes and recreated the old stories, giving the actors themselves replenished costume, mask, and setting. Clearly, through the ages, actual events become embellished or compressed, history shades into tale, lives become legend. We may understand this process as a corruption of history, but would profit more by understanding its creative relevance. With fresh insight offered by new eras of history, each generation draws out and expands the essence of the messages conveyed by the lives and teaching of legendary figures. Emerging out of the mists and permutations of the many versions of ancient myths, the legendary ones shine out convincingly and in renewed clarity as great teachers and mentors.

With its many branches and innumerable roots, myth is full of the fabulous and can change dramatically over time. In general, myth remains a loosely tied net catching large, vaguely related themes which often serve to explain the origins of various phenomena. Though colorful, it lacks a fixed and detailed pattern. But legend is of a somewhat different order. The mesh of its net is knotted more tightly;

it is firm enough to hold more specific details of theme and motivation. With tenuous roots in history, legend is the narrative of a significant event or the action of a figure, which can be told or read—*legere*. A legend is entrusted to someone, an envoy or legate, and thus becomes a legacy. Legendary figures become models, conduits of the wisdom of the ages, to whom we look for guidance. Such figures often contend, in human frailty, against the omnipotence of superior forces—often those of the gods. They must persist against great odds without fury and anger, which debilitate, but armed with determination, singleness of purpose, and long-range commitment. Three such figures are the focus of this study: Prometheus, Orpheus, and Socrates.

Prometheus comes to us from such antiquity that he remains mythical even though he has attained a somewhat legendary status. We will visit him enchained on his craggy prison and hear his story through Aeschylus, the great Greek dramatist. Prometheus endured unbelievable suffering for bringing humankind enlightened intelligence—the gift of fire and with it hope. His fixed and unwavering stance is an expression of a "pure" element, something akin to Greek ideals—rocklike and truly monumental. As a mythical character, Prometheus does not develop or give any sign of experiencing a life cycle, yet his suffering, though beyond our sensory comprehension, is moving and enlists our empathy. It is tantalizing to leave Prometheus immobilized on his crag; the story begs for a conclusion. Even just to free him is not enough—we will seek a fanciful development and ending.

Orpheus, shrouded in myth, may or may not have

actual historicity, but he displays such human dimensions that we can understand him, sympathize with his sorrow, and delight in his achievements. He is elusive, so close to the boundary between myth and reality that we can create an individualized version of him—as indeed artists have done through the years. His closeness to the world of the shaman widens the borders of his potential and the ambiguity of his character. However, his involvement with the mystic rites which bear his name suggests that he was more Greek than Thracian, and more human than not. Patron and promoter of all the arts, Orpheus is celebrated in the burst of artistic genius which was the glory of Greece. With his lyre he symbolizes the power of music and all the arts to revive, from the depths, a vitality and a dedication to art experience. He shared the beautiful, enriching and healing all sentient beings, even the earth herself.

In Socrates we find a fully human being who can be located in time; through his consistent life patterns he became a legendary figure of major proportions. He was a bona fide Athenian citizen, and others who lived during his lifetime have provided reports about his appearance and behavior. We can follow his life cycle in some detail, although, where there is no firm evidence, we are only free to have hunches. Socrates lived and moved and had his being in philosophy: the loving (*philos*) search for wisdom (*Sophia*). His dedication cost him his life. We are privileged to have inherited a discourse carried on with his followers just before his death. Plato elegantly and devotedly offers us the legend and biography of a steadfast mentor, a martyr of great integrity, a seeker after truth.

By reviewing these three legendary personages, and to some extent their mythologizers, I am boldly presuming to view them from my late-twentieth-century standpoint. Being neither a notable Greek scholar, nor great dramatist, nor even an acclaimed artist, I simply offer as credentials a long life as dancer, teacher, craftswoman in the arts, and believer in the healing potential of art experience. I became fascinated by Orpheus because I have had a life-long interest in the way in which the arts incite us in our human development. Young people, and for that matter the rest of us, need the arts—the laws of materials, the demands placed upon us when we try to create something—in order to deepen the development that begins with trust and that requires initiative, industry, and competence.

As some activities have become overstrenuous, I have devoted considerable time to writing. The topics of my books have included a study of the role of beads in history; the life of an artist saint, Saint Francis; and most recently, a review of the relation of the senses to wisdom. A book on the cloth of the Mother Goddess was written in India and published there by the Indian Institute of Design. Two other books, one on aging and vitality and one on activity and growth, were written with my husband and other colleagues.

Weaving with words has not come easily for me. Dancing, doing, making were my ways of saying something. Now Socrates I have always judged to be one who used words powerfully. He could choose and arrange them in such a way that they built bridges over great chasms with ease and guided his audience across. Besides his verbal mastery, he seemed to exemplify a complete mastery of himself—a solidity and self-assurance. This may sound like stoicism, which suggests a lack of affect and some deprivation, but surely Socrates enjoyed himself hugely.

I have been married for sixty-two years to an artist trained in psychoanalysis, and our work together has focused on the development of a psychosocial theory of the life cycle. I am persuaded that the early years of life are enormously significant for the foundation of human development. The importance of this foundation in infancy and childhood has been grossly underestimated. We know well that an injured sapling will probably grow into a malformed tree. Children who have been brutalized in mind, body, or spirit are only with difficulty able to develop the basic trust in parents and social milieu which is mandatory for the strength and support of vital hope and self-confidence. Everything I have learned about life, people, and history has convinced me that the strengths—hope, willpower, and the attributes of the play stage (resilience, empathy, and humor), plus competence, fidelity, love, and care—are the sources of integrity—a sense of I—an existential identity.

I judge experiential wisdom to be the accrued fruit of old age—not assuming that the old are necessarily wise. As one ages, one becomes more interested in endurance and in those capacities so necessary in old age, those that make a life of integrity possible. There is no question that much of what passes for integrity in our culture today is dependent upon good fortune—physical, economical, social. Integrity is in danger of being claimed and owned by the privileged; I am well aware of this. And so I am drawn to a Promethean figure, who holds out against *all* odds, who staunchly displays patience in the face of great physical pain and deprivation. Prometheus embodies, metaphorically, something that we each hope we will be capable of when, bound to the rock of our own lives and lot, we are called upon to endure without losing hope. One is inexorably bound to one's entire life.

These concerns are some of the sturdier threads of the warp on which the tapestry of my life is still being improvised. They constitute my biases—my conscious biases. One additional attribute distinguishes me from the three characters we will be discussing—I am a woman. I am offended and concerned that the strengths and natural survival skills of woman, which often rest in her procreativity and in her care for the weak and underprivileged, remain so undervalued in the organization and control of the social order. Athena, once revered throughout the Mediterranean area as the divinity of the hearth and honored for her capacities to nourish creativity and to bind the family and the community in mutuality, is manipulated in the heroic Greek era to serve in the new domain of the masculine. Forced into armor, degraded by unnatural birth, she presides over a patriarchal society with a man's, a warrior's, competitive drive for dominance at home, in the community, and in the world. Centuries later, men still call the shots, be they bullets, missiles, or bombs; the homeless and hungry abound.

Despite their patriarchal milieu, each of our three central characters is guided in essential decisions by womanly figures who shine out persistently and powerfully—Themis, Peitho, Sophia. Themis, an earth goddess of great antiquity, was older, wiser, and less limited than the Olympian gods and goddesses. She hovered over the earth at its formation and guided its patterned ways. Like the Furies and the Fates, she presided over earth's creatures, both animal and human. The snake is her lowly but powerful symbol. Sophia was and is the ancient goddess of wisdom. Known through history and throughout the world by many names, she leads one toward the ripe wisdom of experience that opens understanding and fosters growth, perspective, and clarity.

The earth goddesses and Sophia are fairly well known to us, at least by name, as are Prometheus, Orpheus, and Socrates. Along with these I will introduce a less-known figure: Peitho. For the Greeks in their need to mythologize and visualize important attributes, "persuasion" was embodied by this Olympian goddess, the daughter of Aphrodite, goddess of love, and Ares, god of war. Ares' and Aphrodite's roles encompassed a wide spectrum of potential action and expression, and Peitho's power included the lowest and most sordid as well as the noblest and highest aspects of both of her parents' attributes. Combat can be carried out as vicious slaughter or with noble restraint. Love can be degraded to greedy lust or aspire to inclusive and compassionate *agape*. This far-reaching spectrum, then, is Peitho's heritage. Mortals are notably prone to all these potentials, and thus Peitho may well be considered one of the most human of the gods.

As her name implies, Peitho masters all the po-

tentials of the persuasive skills. She inherited a gift
of tone and expression that makes her captivatingly
irresistible. The Greeks sought her out as indispen-
sable to the pursuit of winning an argument and to
courting with the seductive arts of enticement. But
nowhere is her guidance and presence more consistently needed than in community and international
relations. And nowhere is she more aptly felt than
in the universal response to art, which wordlessly
communicates with all sentient beings and even with
inanimate matter.

Gifted and dedicated as our three primary figures
were, I will contend that without the blessing and
support of this less-known Olympian goddess,
Peitho, they would never have made their messages
so clear, resounding, and memorable. They became
conduits of the wisdom which they bequeathed to
us because they were able to *persuade*. This is a skill
of such importance that without it all offerings and
communication remain inert, dull, and unappealing.
As we pursue the legacies of the subjects of this
book, we will try to highlight Peitho's role and her
power in guiding their lives and decisions.

In idiosyncratic, single-minded, and committed
ways, Prometheus, Orpheus, and Socrates lived out
their convictions. Stubborn dedication to their values
cost them their freedom—even life itself, the ultimate protest. Yet, by so doing, they fashioned their
own immortality. Consider how our heroes have
imprinted themselves on our minds, on our imaginations: Prometheus helplessly chained to a barren
crag at the end of the world, disdaining verbal battle
with Force and Might; Orpheus attacked by crazed

maenads and killed, his lyre soaring up into the sky and his singing head floating down the river to the sea; Socrates, after an impassioned discourse, quietly drinking the hemlock, surrounded by his students. What memorable scenes, what lasting victories, we record through legend's eye.

Each did leave behind a legacy. Prometheus literally embodied the power of persuasion in his patient hope that, with firm commitment, justice without force may prevail. Orpheus lived the conviction that music, song, makes the dullest earth green and that its persuasive vitality is a creative, transcendent recourse to the constant suffering of loss. He teaches us that the persuasion of communication, via the well-chosen, moving word and all the other arts, is an essential source of bonding mutuality. Socrates dedicated himself to sharpening the mind's keen edge. He vigorously freed the pathway to clear thinking from tangled assumptions and thorny prejudgments, so that we may discriminate between the false and the true, separate the good and noble from the base, and above all revere the Idea, that polestar which gives our creativity wings for flight.

Other guides have added warmth, empathy, care, and love to these values which empower enduring relationship in community living. But I am persuaded that these early mentors remain potent, icon-like symbols who sustain, encourage, and light the way.

Though we do all share one home and a com-
monality of human experience, we express our
common journey through an infinite variety of cultural sets and tonalities, each culture shaping the legends and stories it bequeaths to us through its own
particular vision and comprehension of the world.
In addition to understanding the larger mythic patterns and essential strivings exemplified by our three
legendary figures, it is important to appreciate the
unique and fertile soil from which they sprang. Let
us then venture briefly back into that land, and light,
and spirit which was ancient Greece.

I believe that when most people think of Greece
—of the hilly land, the islands and the seas that surround her—they become aware of a special aura that
suffuses sky, land, and water. So it surely must have
been when Greek civilization was at its most brilliant. The radiance still lingers in the remaining ruins
of her splendid works of art. She produced and nourished great historians, philosophers, and statesmen
who still influence us today. We pride ourselves on
following in Greek footsteps as we contemplate the

birth of democratic ideals and principles in that long-ago world. But most of all, we are won by the glorious outburst of creative activity—the festivals, rituals, theater, and the great Olympic Games that bound the world of Greek states together in harmony and devotion to beauty.

Over the shining land of heroic Greece presided the Olympian deities who were immortal, physically perfect, and powerful. They gathered, fully formed, on their mountain home under the auspices of Zeus, a self-appointed sovereign. They experienced no childhood, no development, just never-ending youth, hovering over an unspoiled world with myths for history. Often vexed with one another, they gave considerable attention to mortals, especially when appropriately venerated by them in temples and propitiated in ceremony and sacrifice. Being autonomous and omnipotent, though unable to completely override the ur-old laws of nature, they played important roles in human affairs, while often operating at cross-purposes with fellow gods and goddesses.

Though never actually seen, the immortals were so vividly imagined by human beings that their existence was rarely questioned. Each god or goddess embodied a particular Greek ideal, the essence of various human aspirations. Unlike a human being, who has to deal with conflicting attributes and drives—devotion and jealousy, generosity and greed, pride and humility—a god could be serene and perfect in the single aspect for which he or she served as archetype. Dazzling in their physical perfection, the gods inspired the Greeks to portray them in their beauty and to construct temples and sculpture of a natural grace and form that have rarely, if ever, been equaled.

For the peasant, villager, laborer, and slave, the gods provided a wealth of material for mythological tales of their affairs and dealings with mortals. These stories gave shape and meaning to the forces with which humans cope daily. They made sense of what seemed gratuitous and beyond control. The unpredictable could be made more sensible, tangible, acceptable. Someone or something was in charge and could possibly be approached for direction or assistance. One could propitiate, succeed, and celebrate gratefully without excessive pride—that human pitfall, especially frowned upon by the gods.

Yet, in many ways the Olympian gods, being awesome in their grandeur, were unapproachable. For the peasant in his hayfield or vineyard these great ones were remote, too far away and fine for the sweaty laborer eking a living out of his work. More accessible were the nature gods and goddesses and spirits inhabiting the countryside, the mountains and forests, living in the trees and stones, fields and rivers. They enlivened nature and were close to humankind. Among these demigods were Chiron the centaur, part man and part horse; bearded Pan the flute-playing deity with goat feet and horns; and the nymphs, dryads, and satyrs. These earth-dwelling lesser gods enriched life with their presence, increasing the wonder and significance of the natural world—an animated world full of potential surprises: a tree swaying in the wind could be a nymph dancing or beckoning; a bird sings, or is it Pan with his sweet piping? Pan is the playful one to whom Socrates, on a country outing, prayerfully appealed:

Aphrodite, with the help of Eros, playfully threatens goat-footed Pan with her sandal.

"Beloved Pan and all ye deathless gods who here abide—Grant me to be beautiful in the inner man, and all I have of outer things to be at peace with those within."[2] A rock then added reverently to a nearby peasant herm, or shrine, could sanctify such a special spot in a delight-giving world of awareness and wonder.

Here, then, is the peaceable kingdom of beneficent spirits where spring and harvest times prevail, and human beings live in harmony with themselves and one another—the great myth of all times. Alas, not so—for we know well that there are grievous inequalities. Some humans have much, some have little; there is deformity, sickness; the life span varies. Inevitably there is loss—nothing endures and time leads to old age; death blots out and then one joins the shades. How does a man make his mark, claim a notation in the memory scroll of the future? The Greek answer, it seems, was to become a hero, perform a feat worthy of being remembered. Women, on the whole, had no such presumptions or ambitions, although their gravestones could and sometimes did boast the posthumous acclaim of male heroes.

In an era of city-states there were boundaries to guard against encroaching neighbors—neighbors with ideas of expansion, and young heroes ready to show their prowess. First with wood, leather, and stone, their arms were extended and strengthened and their bodies protected. Then came the discovery and the forging of metals into arms and shields. The building of boats stretched the horizon. The clashing of metals—cymbals and weapons—and the rhythmic beat of marching feet were, and still are, all-compelling, exciting sounds that rouse energy and pulse. Adventure beckons and young heroes are off to make names for themselves and prove their metal. The city folk respond with enthusiasm, country folk marvel and cheer. Artisans cleverly ply their skills; shipwrights become inventive and bold; weavers develop their craft and discover bright dyes and new fibers. The city itself is enlivened with excitement: celebrations, arrivals and departures, the elaborate and beloved festivals, and always the propitiations and acclamations of the gods. It is the heroic age of Athens, of Greece—not unlike the present.

How else did a young fellow become a hero in ancient Greece? It was best, no doubt, to be "the son of" an outstanding citizen, a person of status who could afford to give a young son an appropriate education and training. Physical strength, skills of dexterity and endurance, and gymnastics, which would develop the whole body harmoniously, were all mandatory. This involved consistent and arduous training—competitive sports and games and, finally, enlistment in the games and trials of the Olympiad. Such a great event offered another way to rate as hero. Olympic heroes became models for sculptors, and were hailed, applauded, and housed in splendid quarters in Athens. This tremendous festival, held every fourth year in honor of Zeus, included all Greece, and took place on a wide plain at Olympia, in Elis, dedicated to this purpose. It included all manner of contests which provided clues as to what composed a young Greek male's education.

Our present-day Olympic Games give us some idea of the prestige and the concentrated effort involved for those taking part in the contests. Unfortunately, unlike the Greeks, we do not include the arts, mathematics, or rhetoric. In a democracy, one should be able to speak well in order to express one's views and opinions clearly. Training in rhetoric was sought and debate practiced as a necessary skill. Young men attached themselves to respected teachers, listened, asked questions, and argued. And why do we not include the arts in our Olympics? All the arts are realized, actualized, by means of the body; energy is a property of the whole body, and we are diminished by such arbitrary selectivity.

Clearly all of the necessary training could be done only if the young individual was not earning his living or supporting a family. The process was selective and highly competitive, a motivation which we have inherited. A large segment of the population was, of course, excluded from this upbringing: the peasants, farmers, and slaves, not to mention women, provided a basic continuity when the would-be young heroes set off seeking acclaim, adventure, and heroism.

Also among the nonlaboring class were the philosophers, whose aspirations were neither warlike nor like those of the Olympic heroes, although in their youth they, too, might have served as valiant soldiers. How did they relate to the young, beautiful, unchanging gods and goddesses? Were these archetypes compelling or really useful? All citizens were required to be involved in the polis, in the education of their children, and in all community affairs; what guidance or inspiration could carefree, autonomous, postadolescent gods offer? Perhaps Zeus had "developed" venerability, and Demeter was, and always

Theater at Delphi.

had been, a mother goddess. But none of the gods had directly experienced taking part in the maintenance of the social order, in caring for the less advantaged. Nor had they experienced aging—the loss of physical strength, beauty, skill, and mental sharpness, and resulting loss of self-confidence. As the philosophers tried to pinpoint values necessary for the stability of the social structure and the polis, and to define virtues such as honor, truth, and morality, it became increasingly difficult to hope for any guidance from the lofty characters which the popular state religion offered as supportive models and revered archetypes.

There were strict and vigorously enforced laws against impiety. Aeschylus was accused of having revealed the Eleusinian mysteries in a dramatic production. He pled that he was unaware of the breach of secrecy, and he was acquitted, they say, not because of his defense, but because of his heroic participation as warrior in the Persian Wars. There were many such trials, negative decisions, and grave penalties. The law was basic: the state did not permit discussion, derision, or questioning of the Olympic gods. Athens was flourishing under their jurisdiction; no one was permitted to challenge their supremacy, their Zeus-given right to reverence and homage.

Even so, a sense of the divine, a sense of order in the universe under the auspices of a supreme deity, seems to have prevailed over and beyond the state definitions. A pantheon of young, perfect, and irresponsible gods did not provide the leeway of thought necessary for an emerging ideal government. How did the divine right of the rather arbitrary thunderbolt thrower, Zeus, fit into the struggling new order? "Democracy," a new energizing idea, an approach to government by the people, was taking form. Something young and fresh was alive in Greece and most alive in Athens. With a spirit of discovery in the polis, a demand for a voice in the management of the social order had asserted itself. This new vigor was exemplified by such statesmen as Solon, whose legal code opposing tyranny and injustice laid the constitutional foundations of Athenian democracy; and Pericles, considered the greatest of all Athenians, whose democratic reforms transformed Athens and brought it to its peak of power.

The populace in general needed nurturance and involvement of another, even deeper kind. Mortals experienced birth, health and fitness as designated by the Fates, the mysteries of nature, death according to the dictates of destiny, and then Hades. This script suggests dreariness and drudgery, and no one can deny the reality of this aspect of fate, but there are also moments of elation and awe. Where did the common people find expression for the divine in their lives? Surely ritual, festival, and community celebration were and still are the outlets for this need. The laborers could escape the repetitious dullness of routine through myths embedded in their theater, poetry, music, and song, close to nature that surrounded them, and to the hearth and the heart. All the creative arts are an expression of the divine; rising above rigidified state religious doctrine, they offer a way toward the sublime—the lodestar of every true artist, Beauty.

There was theater, not only the extant construc-
tions themselves, in their expectant stillness, but the
great tragedies and hilarious comedies—legacies we
have inherited, some in their entireties and some in
fragments. Was there ever again such theater, theater
for everyone as a living, nourishing gift to community life? What incredible riches! With theater, of
course, but also at all festivals, there was music and
dance. It is sad that their musical notation now exists
only in fragments and that no sound was recorded,
sad that we will never know details about Greek
dance or see it as actually performed in ancient times.

The supreme legacy of Greece was her artists.
Masters of the plastic arts flourished in Athens,
where their work was revered and displayed for all
to see. Such names as Praxiteles, Alcamenes, Ke-
phisodotus, and Pheidias are immortalized in marble.
We marvel at the skill of their workmanship, at the
Greek vision of the human form in its perfection and
the subtlety of graceful motion caught in stone. Such
sculpture was displayed in city buildings, the forum,
and the baths, and in small and large temples, the
artistry of which in form and workmanship has
rarely been approximated. The visual glories of what
was once Greece, the lovely traces that can still be
seen, are silencing.

There were consummate craftsmen, too, who prepared the clay in time-honored ways and then
formed and embellished all manner of pots, bowls,
cups, and large vessels for storage. The paintings on
these are still full of the brilliant color which bright-
ened a civilization of which we now see only remnants in museum displays. Of course, no one ever

saw the gods. Only the artists portrayed their beauty and perfection; they created visions in materials, designs, and color of lasting vitality.

Whereas the manifested gods were the creation of these supreme craftsmen, the myths—the themes that had increased their potency and mystery through their retelling over the centuries—were the creation of gifted storytellers, the epic poets and dramatists. The magnificent Homer, gave us the Olympian gods in their most glorious forms: gray-eyed Athena, wise and regal; Apollo, brilliant in his fiery chariot; Artemis, moon goddess and protectress of the shy deer and playful nymphs; Hermes, the active, quixotic messenger of the gods; and the irresistibly lovely Aphrodite. Only inspired poetry could do justice to their splendor and the freshness of their beauty. Without the legacy of Homeric poetry, and that of the later poets, these immortals might have remained dully inactive and merely decorative. How impoverished Greece would have been without the *Iliad* and the *Odyssey*, the fragments that remain from Musaeus and Hesiod, and the wealth of art which Orpheus fathered! When we consider that, as is reckoned, only one-fifth of the writing and art of Greece has survived, we realize that their productivity must have been beyond our dreaming.

Hellas, that glorious land of long ago, we visit in our imaginations and keep alive empathically in spirit. While clearly there was poverty, illness, and deformity—not to mention the subjugation of women, slavery, and great cruelty—the brilliance of the beauty and the height of the philosophic truths cast such a glow that knowing the darker facts does not obscure the glory and appeal of ancient Greece. We claim it as political, intellectual ancestor and do homage to the iconlike envoys whom we treasure and would emulate. Let us turn our attention to Prometheus, Orpheus, and Socrates.

Prometheus

We are in Athens in the great amphitheater pressed into the side of a hill—the original city site no doubt chosen with this in mind. Picture the scene: tier on tier of stone slabs hauled into place, half surrounding a space open for action. The people arrive in festive mood, piling in to fill every seat. It is barely daylight; the dusk before dawn, as solemn as the dusk before nightfall, casts long shadows. At a signal, great quiet falls. No intrusive machine-age sounds are audible —nothing disturbs the immense silence of a world without industrial technology. Then a voice begins to speak, a chorus to intone some of the most beautiful poetry ever composed. The actors move through the scenes, the drama unfolds. The audience laughs at the ludicrous, weeps at terror and pain, acknowledging the human plight, yet exalted by the power of men and women to suffer and die nobly, thus transcending fate with grandeur.

This then is Greece, the theater, the setting of the great dramas we have inherited and been moved by through the centuries. Our imaginary audience has just viewed a performance of Aeschylus' *Prometheus*

Bound. Toward the close of his life, this great tragedian wrote a trilogy of which *Prometheus Bound* was the first part. Unfortunately, parts two and three of this trilogy are lost; only fragments remain. In the pages which follow, "Prometheus Unbound," a twentieth-century version of Prometheus' release from bondage, will be presented in an attempt to offset this loss. First, however, a review of Aeschylus' *Prometheus Bound* is offered to provide background and to clarify the themes developed. Program notes are also offered concerning Aeschylus and Greek theater, as is information about the central characters portrayed in *Prometheus Bound*. Both of these plays are based on an ancient myth about suffering and enduring hope—a myth well known to all Greeks of the fifth century B.C.

Background of the Myth

Our myth begins at the end of the reign of Cronus. There has been a furious battle between Zeus and the other Titans for control of the world. The fighting is now over and the battle is as won as any battle ever is. Zeus, the victor, has banished Cronus, his father, along with the great Titans, his brothers, to the depths of Tartarus. The eternal gods have gathered on Olympus, and Zeus presides over them and the cosmos.

However, not all of the Titans have been allotted the general fate of banishment. The mighty Atlas is forced to bend his head, to carry on his shoulders and support with his hands the great weight of the sky and heavens above. Hephaestus, master of the depths of the earth and skilled craftsman of forging metals, crippled by a thunderbolt, is in servile bondage to Zeus. Typho, he of explosive nature-energy, lies sprawled out and buried beneath Mount Aetna, making known his angry presence with groans and rumbling from time to time. And Prometheus, formerly an ally of Zeus and the Olympian gods, is being punished cruelly for what, in Zeus' judgment, was a presumptuous and arrogant act. Prometheus, the hero—or should one say nonhero—of the myth, has stolen fire from the gods and given it to humankind.

Prometheus' father was the god Uranus, his mother the primeval earth deity Themis, "of wise counsel." Themis, known to us also as Gaia, preceded the era of the Olympian gods; she presided over the earth's natural forces during the reign of her father, Cronus, when Destiny, the Fates, and the Furies oversaw the affairs of humankind. Although Prometheus was thus part god, his natural empathy was drawn to humankind. Themis no doubt made Prometheus observant of earthly things and compassionate toward poorly endowed creatures. Zeus mistrusted mortals and had considered ridding the world of human beings altogether. But Prometheus had seen how richly endowed wild animals were with their tough hides and glossy pelts, which offered warmth and protection. Theirs also were long, sharp claws, great muscles for climbing and running, and shiny fangs for tearing apart vegetation and meat. The naked, upright, and vulnerable humans with their underdeveloped sensory perceptions were hopelessly defenseless against such hungry predators. The lives of these humans were miserable and their fate, he felt, unjust.

Prometheus responded to this injustice, and, although he knew he was in danger, cleverly, perhaps craftily, stole fire from the gods and gave it to mortals. With this great gift came enlightenment, for humans were endowed with brain potential. They became practical and skillful in the processes of making and doing, building and preserving. Prometheus also gave these "creatures of a day" hope—blind hope—a trust that life is essentially beneficent despite mortal helplessness.

But, in response to Prometheus' deeds, the Olympian gods are angry. Zeus is furious and vindictive; he does not tolerate hubris, even in demigods.

The Myth as Presented by Aeschylus

Prometheus Bound opens with a scene of Prometheus being dragged by Hephaestus and Zeus' ruthless minions, Kratos (Might) and Bia (Force), to a remote and barren crag in the Caucasus, which only winged creatures may reach. These servile henchmen bind Prometheus' feet and arms with iron chains to this massive rock at the end of the world, and they hammer a metal spike through his chest, rendering him immobile. To add to his torture, a black vulture will visit daily to tear apart and feast on his liver. There will be no end to this misery, since Prometheus is a demigod and immortal.

Next the birdlike daughters of Oceanus, Prometheus' father-in-law, having heard the clang of bronze being hammered, fly up from their deep watery caverns to the craggy heights above them to discover the cause. They flutter around the prisoner and commiserate with him in chorus as he explains the charge against him:

PROMETHEUS
I rescued men from shattering destruction . . . and therefore I am tortured on this rock. . . . I caused mortals to cease foreseeing doom.

CHORUS
What cure did you provide them with against their sickness?

PROMETHEUS
I placed in them blind hopes.

CHORUS
That was a great gift you gave to men.

PROMETHEUS
Besides this, I gave them fire.

CHORUS
And do creatures of a day now possess bright-faced fire?

PROMETHEUS
Yes, and from it they shall learn many crafts.[1]

Prometheus describes at great length just what benefactions he has bestowed on mortals. He passionately paints for his visitors a bleak picture of the predicament of humankind before he came to their rescue. No doubt he wishes to justify his defiant action and enlist the sympathy of his visitors:

I found them witless and gave them the use of their
wits and made them masters of their minds. . . . For
men at first had eyes but saw to no purpose; they had
ears but did not hear. Like the shapes of dreams they
dragged through their long lives and handled all things
in bewilderment and confusion. They did not know
of building houses with bricks to face the sun; they
did not know how to work in wood. They lived like
swarming ants in holes in the ground, in the sunless
caves of the earth. . . . It was I who made visible to
men's eyes the flaming signs of the sky that were before
dim. So much for these. Beneath the earth, man's hidden blessing, copper, iron, silver, and gold—will anyone claim to have discovered these before I did? . . .
It was I and none other who discovered ships, the sail-
driven wagons that the sea buffets. Such were the con-
trivances that I discovered for men—alas for me! For
I myself am without contrivance to rid myself of my
present affliction.[2]

Obviously Prometheus was an enthusiastic teacher,
and human beings were apt students. The listening
Athenian audience must have been as fascinated by
a recital of the development of their technical expertise as we are of ours today. It is noteworthy that
in this whole long, formidable list no mention is
made of any hope for harmony, justice, and peace.

Oceanus, who has flown up to the crag on the
back of his seabird, is more concerned with other
matters. In a fatherly fashion, he tries to persuade
Prometheus to mollify Zeus, but Prometheus is convinced that the new king is angry and vindictive.
Prometheus will not give in: "This cup I shall drain
myself till the high mind of Zeus shall cease from

anger."[3] His foreknowledge tells him that the tyrannical Zeus cannot escape what is fated; only Prometheus knows that this shortsighted supreme god will misplan in such a way as to cause his own inevitable downfall. He declares, in fact, that newly empowered tyrants like Zeus, in their insecurity, usually overreact with panic to any real or imagined threat. We remember that Zeus mistrusted humankind and the threat of their potential. Foresight, which is the meaning of his name, is deepened in Prometheus, we note, by a rare capacity for psychological insight.

When Prometheus next receives a brief visit from Io with her horned and winged cowlike body, he is moved with pity for the suffering which jealous Hera, Zeus' wife, has inflicted on her. Io's inflated body is pregnant with a child of Zeus, and a horde of biting flies forces her to move constantly without rest. Poor, long-suffering Io must endure such misery until she is able to bear the child she carries and be released from constant torment. Does her contact with Prometheus—that symbol of renewing hope—fortify her? Did Themis, the earth mother, guide her there? Io's child will be the ancestor of a hero, another child of Zeus, who, some generations hence, will bring release to Prometheus. But the name and immediate parentage of this descendant demigod is known only to Prometheus.

In addition, only Prometheus knows what woman will bear the god destined to overthrow Zeus, and he will guard this secret through as many generations as will be necessary for the fruition of the prophecy. Zeus, on Mount Olympus, hears their conversation and finally sends Hermes, his messenger, to demand the information that Prometheus has been claiming. Hermes arrives, aloof, patronizing, and threatening:

> You, subtle-spirit, you
> bitterly overbitter, you that sinned
> against the immortals, giving honor to
> the creatures of a day, you thief of fire:
> the Father has commanded you to say
> what marriage of his is this you brag about
> that shall drive him from power—and declare it
> in clear terms and no riddles.[4]

This is the message of a tyrant, and the Greeks had certainly experienced the ruthless power of tyrants. Gathering around them strong-armed henchmen and scorning the democratic process dear to the more sober minds of thoughtful citizens, these tyrants coerced their way into power. With sheer might and violence they assumed control and forced their rule not only on Athens but also on her allies. To be subjugated was painful, but breaking a tyrant's grip cost lives and also brought much misery. To regain the dominance of reason over brute force was a long, painful struggle and included heartbreaking losses.

Prometheus' reply to Hermes is as cool and condescending as the initial threat from Hermes:

> Your speech is pompous sounding, full of pride,
> as fits the lackey of the gods. You are young
> and young your rule and you think that the tower
> in which you live is free from sorrow: from it
> have I not seen two tyrants thrown? the third,
> who now is king, I shall yet live to see him

fall, of all three most suddenly, most dishonored.
Do you think I will crouch before your gods,
—so new—and tremble? I am far from that.
Hasten away, back on the road you came.
You shall learn nothing that you ask of me.[5]

This, then, is the proud answer of the Greek citizen. Intelligence must win out in the struggle between violence and thoughtful, persuasive discourse; the rule of law and order must prevail against mere force.

As Hermes and Prometheus continue their sparring, the scene ends in flashes of lightning and thunder. Zeus has finally thrown the threatened bolt; the boulders crash and fall. Prometheus, chained to his rock, lies half buried. And so the play ends.

The Myth Continues

After generations pass, Zeus falls in love with a mortal, Alcmene, and she bears him a son, Heracles. Alcmene, then, is the long-awaited descendant of Io, and the mother of Heracles, as Prometheus had foreknown. Zeus found mortal women very attractive, and he had many sons and daughters too. He did not know, of course, that this particular son, Heracles, of whom he was very proud, would one day decide to free Prometheus. Indeed, we may well wonder what it was that appealed to Heracles about Prometheus. Was it Prometheus' steadfast fortitude under these worst of circumstances—or perhaps his indomitable hope and patience, inculcated by his earth goddess mother, who presides over the on-going, eon-long processes of global change?

The great martyrs of history die heroically for just causes, and are then immortalized by monuments erected in their honor and acclaimed in verse and song through the ages. Prometheus is a legendary figure who, though never quite forgotten, remains impaled on a rock for generations. We are vaguely told that a rescuer will come and release him. To leave Prometheus, whose integrity we have come to respect, bound helplessly on a bare rock is somehow unacceptable; it becomes imperative to imagine his final release. We can only guess what Aeschylus had in mind, and we must at least know more about Heracles in order to consider his qualifications and potential role.

Heracles, the Ultimate Hero

Heracles was beloved by Zeus, and all the other gods hovered over him with gifts and support. Legends about him abound—he was so excessively adventurous, strong, self-confident, and successful that he has no parallel among the great heroes of Greece. Heracles is a paragon, the archetypal hero. He seems not to be bound to any particular locality; all localities claimed him and no area was able to establish the unequivocal right to serve as his burial place. His name became attached to so many heroic feats that we must assume these legends about him accrued over a long stretch of time.

At Heracles' birth, as the myth is told, Zeus' jealous wife, Hera, put two snakes in his crib, whereupon the infant killed one with each hand. Goaded on by this evasion of her plan, Hera became the archetypal evil stepmother, trying repeatedly to destroy him, while Zeus dotingly supported his fantastic exploits.

When grown, Heracles was eight feet tall and was skillful in the use of all the tools of the hunt and weapons of battle, having been trained by the greatest heroes. However, from early youth he ruthlessly killed any man or beast that stood in his impulsive way. Orpheus' brother, Linus, offended Heracles as he was teaching him to play a song, and Heracles impetuously killed him with the lyre. Claiming self-defense, he was acquitted. Following this, however, in a fit of rage he threw two of his own and two of Iphicles' children into a blazing fire, and for this sin he was committed to serve the king of Mycenae for twelve years performing heroic labors. Most of these adventures were focused on ridding the world of savage animals and monsters—a fact which offers a clue to the antiquity of these tales.

After completing twelve labors, Heracles was forced to expiate further murders in order to be acquitted and purified. Heracles joined one expedition after another, such as the Argonauts' search for the Golden Fleece. Husband of many wives, father of many, many children, and successful in numerous enterprises, he was inexhaustible, but he always seemed to use his strengths, skills, and violence in the service of someone else's goals. In one way he can be seen as a pathetic figure, but for the Greeks he was nonetheless the epitome of heroism. This is the story of humankind, as old as, if not older than, the myths: the end seems to justify the means used to accomplish the task. However, violent means distort the ends and engender more violence and hatred. One purpose of the ancient myths seems to have been to make this utterly clear. Perhaps myths live on because we have, as yet, never learned to live by the truths they tell us. Greece always finally forgave Heracles. In the heroic age of fifth-century-B.C. Greece, success was blinding.

We will probably never know what Aeschylus actually developed in parts two and three of his trilogy. Are there any clues to how Aeschylus might have cast a hero who, in all his behavior, acted out a completely negative script—a script in utter contrast to Apollo's dictum as inscribed on his temple in Delphi, "Nothing too much," or, in another version, "Nothing in excess"?[6] We have learned to accept this wisdom as intrinsic to the "harmony in all things" of the ancient Greece we acclaim. Heracles, whose approach was violent action, might well be at a loss addressing and conversing with Prometheus, the immobilized savior and teacher of humankind. If Aeschylus' plan, as the fragments suggest, was for Heracles to become a benefactor of humans, what would he have promoted? Perhaps, by the time of his release, Prometheus' hindsight and foresight would have clarified for him how he could guide Heracles. There is no hint of why Heracles comes to free Prometheus. But Aeschylus must have had some strategy to bind two such disparate characters—the charismatic, steadfast stoic and the impetuous, ultimate hero—into a creative team.

Heracles had never been happy with his extraordinary life. Successes had only resulted in penalties and forced expiation. Since his major achievements were superhuman and always supported by the gods, perhaps he had never really come to terms with the loving and caring, human elements in his nature. Original empathy and mutuality may have been difficult to establish with his human mother, who had been forced to cope with snakes in his crib and with the constant intrusion of god-given powers and directions to her son. But Heracles must have had a potential for such caring, for he does undertake the arduous labor of seeking out Prometheus on his remote mountain crag, where he then kills the vulture, and releases Prometheus from his chains. No one seems to have instigated this course of action; it was Heracles' own idea.

We can only guess how Aeschylus planned to focus Heracles' arrogantly aggressive propensities and dangerously insolent human pride in collaboration with Prometheus in his continued service to humankind. Perhaps Heracles could be persuaded that violence and ruthlessness are, in the long run, neither viable nor enduring. Heroic qualities inculcated for purposes of making the world a more harmonious and creative place in which to develop interdependence might become Heracles' and Prometheus' common concern and commitment.

Could we conjecture that Aeschylus envisioned a state and social order where heroic enthusiasm would be focused on human growth and social skills? Aeschylus would surely have extended this ideal state to the whole world and its many parts in all their mysterious otherness. Communication, transportation, free trade, cultural interrelationships—he would have applauded all these. Aeschylus did not write about trivial matters. What, in his old age, did he have in mind to teach his countrymen and us? We stand to gain by understanding this great dramatist, for in this way we may clarify the meaning of the myth and our own relationship to it. We must now turn our attention to Aeschylus in order to even presume to guess how the plot might develop—to glean his values, loves and hates.

Aeschylus and Greek Theater

Aeschylus was dramatically able to make Prometheus come to life by giving him voice and by making this voice persuasive. Since it was a customary practice in fifth-century-B.C. Athens, it is more than probable that Aeschylus himself enacted the role of Prometheus in the first production, and was thus truly in command of the performance.

Statements about this prolific dramatist in the written works of his contemporaries offer a few facts which place him in historical perspective. Aeschylus died in 456 B.C. at the age of about seventy, which makes 525 B.C. his approximate year of birth. His family lived in Eleusis and were esteemed members of the wealthy nobility. This small city near Athens was the distinguished center of the Eleusinian mysteries, and it is recorded that Aeschylus deeply revered Demeter, goddess of earth and fertility. Prometheus' mother, Themis, an even more ancient earth goddess, no doubt shared his reverence.

Aeschylus lived in the period of Greek history when Athens was at the high point of its greatness. During his lifetime, the tyrant Hippias had been expelled from Athens in a "glorious revolution," which had made possible the early victories of democratic government. The Persian Wars had ended in two great defeats of Persia, and the peace which followed made possible a powerful Greece and the founding and expansion of the Athenian empire. Aeschylus had actually participated in a praiseworthy manner in the war and in the revolution, and he took pride in the new democracy and freedom that had been won. He writes proudly in *The Persians* of the Athenians as subject and slave to no man. It was a buoyant, hopeful period in Athens in which to be a tragic dramatist and to present one's work to enthusiastic audiences who shared fundamental principles and high ideals. Life seemed to support the optimistic assumption that in the long run, the better cause might be expected to prevail, thus justifying intense effort, suffering, and heroism.

Like other Greek men and Athenians in particular, Aeschylus admired and revered heroism, complete "body-on-the-line" devotion to a challenge or cause. It is probable that he had grown up as a great admirer of Heracles, that epitome of the daring warrior and overcomer of all obstacles. But in time, as an old man, he may have deplored the violence and impulsiveness of the hero, while still being drawn to the thrill and excitement that empower a young man to throw himself completely into winning the day. A conviction—that youthful enthusiasm is, in itself, intrinsically good, of the gods, and should be preserved when channeled into peaceful pursuits of benefit to humankind—might have prompted him to try to link Heracles with the bound, but determined Prometheus.

The heroic mode had for centuries been the road

to fame, to recognition, and to the final achievement of acclaim as a valiant Greek. Aeschylus was therefore understandably proud of his own youthful martial prowess. His tomb bears an inscription glorifying his military valor:

> This tomb the dust of Aeschylus doth hide,
> Euphorion's son, and fruitful Gela's pride.
> How tried his valour Marathon may tell,
> And long-haired Medes who knew it all too well.[7]

Since the inscription does not mention his victories as a tragic dramatist, which would have been alluded to by anyone else, but only his heroism in battle, it is presumed that he himself wrote it. If this is true, it is wonderfully and appropriately dramatic. He, the truly great poet and dramatist, at seventy, writes his own final lines and draws attention to his once youthful zest and his nostalgic attraction to the heroic mode.

One may pause to marvel at the fact that after more than 2,400 years it is still possible to read many of the dramatic works of this playwright, Aeschylus, realizing too that much more has been lost. Something must have encouraged the Greeks to feel that the value of their writings would endure and that the record of the lives of great men would enrich history. Did they believe that Greece was called upon to play a unique, exemplary role, and did the Athenians in particular feel themselves to be a "chosen people"— their history, their mythology, in a sense, also a special source of wisdom? Some such mission seems to pervade the preserved written record of their civilization.

Given the role that theater played in fifth-century-B.C. Greece, it is impossible to rate too highly the influence of the innovative dramatic artists. Their interpretation of ancient myths transformed them into sources of accrued wisdom and threw light on the immediate, puzzling history of present affairs. Whereas, to the delight of the citizenry, Greek comedy often dealt with current local events and even politics, the great dramas and tragedies were based on mythology. Petty themes did not claim time or interest. Respect for the role of the dramatist demanded that the themes be lofty and ethically instructive. In Greek drama, a fusion of artistry and religion takes place which enhances both and gives the moral laws of the universe precedence.

In Aeschylus' plays, destiny and providence display their power through the actors' behavior, which is invested with grandeur and strength, serving to inspire nobility and virtue. Oppression is to be resisted, generous devotion to humanity to be earnestly emulated. Aeschylus celebrates the virtues of fairness, arbitration, justice, and law-abiding devotion to cautious democracy, which safeguard against the anarchy resulting from too much popular control. He tends to curb the more ancient forces of mythology, the wildness of the Furies and the violence of the Titans, yet he maintains respect for destiny and allows time for the development of due process and judgment. The unfolding of the drama, as one would expect, also demonstrates that actions have inevitable consequences, that insolent pride—hubris—will be punished by the gods. Justice, though its processes may be slow, will in the end be fulfilled. As Aeschylus writes in the *Agamemnon*,

"Justice so moves that those only learn who suffer; and the future you shall know when it has come. . . ."[8] This justice, however, must be tempered by mercy to override law as the situation demands.

While in many of Aeschylus' plays Zeus is presented as a model of justice, in *Prometheus Bound* he is portrayed more as an oppressive tyrant, insecure in his new office and mistrustful even of former collaborators. This shift or inconsistency seems to point to a reevaluation of Zeus' character, or perhaps it reflects Aeschylus' perception of changes in his own milieu. Premonition may have warned him that when unjust tyrants are in charge, the natural world suffers and all hope for peaceful existence and harmonious relationship within the social system is jeopardized. Aeschylus himself lived his final years away from vainglorious Athens, where war, rebellion, and expansion kept life in turmoil, where there were upheavals, major calamities, and constant threats to and from uncooperative vassal states, and where all the challenged, oppressed, and defeated hated the bully and waited, hankering after revenge. How familiar! How depressing!

Aeschylus' plays suggest that he considered his role to be that of teacher and mentor to his audience. Aeschylus was aging—seventy years was a venerable old age in those times—but he did live to write the two final sections of his Promethean trilogy. This trilogy, developed in a hope-filled direction, was perhaps to be his legacy to a less violent future. Probably every old person, knowing that death is unavoidably and appropriately coming close, would wish to sum up a lifetime of experiential learning in one significant act, one ripe statement or dramatic presentation. Perhaps that was initially the opportunity that gravestones were intended to offer. For a seasoned writer and dramatist a play carries such a message much more effectively and memorably. How enriched we might have been had we inherited the final sections of Aeschylus' trilogy in their entirety.

Hope

Early in *Prometheus Bound* when the seabird-like daughters of Oceanus ask Prometheus what he did to deserve Zeus' anger, he says: "I gave to mortal man a precedence over myself in pity. . . . I caused mortals to cease foreseeing doom. . . . I placed in them blind hopes. . . . Besides this, I gave them fire."[9] Although Prometheus mentions hope, as well as pity and compassion, *before* fire, no further reference is made in the play to these initial gifts. He describes at great length the excellence of the benefits of fire and what it has done for humankind, but he offers no detailed account of the virtues of hope except that it is the remedy for despair. Thus, although Aeschylus does give hope a place of importance, he does not underscore it in *Prometheus Bound*.

It remains puzzling that Prometheus should have had the power to bestow the gift of hope; "foreknowledge" does not necessarily ensure hope. Perhaps what Prometheus offered humankind was the basic survival strength of hope, like that of the infant who is welcomed into this world with loving care, a truly blind hope. What does a newborn creature do to express its hope, to demand the attention necessary for its survival? The tiny animal squeaks and nuzzles its mother for warmth and nourishment. The human infant cries out, that cry forcing a first breath of life into its ready lungs. The mother responds out of an equally compelling need to have, hold, and protect the newborn. For the infant there is one source, the mother or surrogate. For most individuals, a constant yearning for a Source is lifelong.

Let us assume that Prometheus' earth goddess mother, who presides over natural forces, rhythms, and seasons, was *his* source. Nature, though sometimes cruel, is constantly optimistic, generative, and therefore less despairing than humankind. Proceeding with a creative reproductive cycle—dependable, generous, equally abundant for the just and the unjust—she rarely fails or falters. She heralds the year's pattern with her seasonal splendor, and her lavish bounty persuades us that productivity is her goal. Where else would one look for the source of hope?

We often use the word "hope" casually, with little consideration for what it means, what it promises, and how it supports life. It has been singled out as the one mandatory strength, beyond protection from the elements, that a human infant must have in order to survive. Throughout the life cycle it continues to be the vital strength, the lifeline for positive development and growth. Without it, motivation is lifeless and inert, inspiration is negligible, and creativity impossible. This initial hope of the infant is a gift of the procreative process.

Prometheus, incredibly, succeeded in maintaining hope through centuries of suffering. A fundamental hope, supported by sensory awareness and an acceptance of the reliability of nature, had obviously been established early in his life. This hope could then be shared with all sentient beings in empathy and, as Prometheus himself says, "pity." The long list of what, under his aegis, mortals were to achieve is ample evidence of the energy he was willing to share in the processes involved. Barred from this effort by Zeus, he focused his total energy on observing, foreseeing, and enduring. Themis must have maintained his superhuman energy; she had not failed to convince her son of her trustworthiness and of his own capacity to survive.

Regardless of his bitterness and anger, and despite the brutality of his punishment, Prometheus' confidence in Zeus, whom he had once served, is without parallel. He maintains a belief in the potential of this supreme god to be "softened." Early in *Prometheus Bound*, Prometheus spells out confidently and in detail, to the chorus of seabirds, just how Zeus will change and relent:

> I know that he is savage: and his justice
> a thing he keeps by his own standard: still
> that will of his shall melt to softness yet
> when he is broken in the way I know,
> and though his temper now is oaken hard
> it shall be softened: hastily he'll come
> to meet my haste, to join in amity
> and union with me—one day he shall come.[10]

Prometheus is patiently, stolidly determined to wait, his defenseless body outstretched and chained to a rock—a supreme symbol of constancy and enduring faith.

This image of Prometheus is what should be celebrated and honored in awe and wonder. In our present-day world, Prometheus is portrayed in sculpture in Rockefeller Center, on the Yale campus, and elsewhere, and always with a torch, celebrating his gift of light and power. Is there such a tribute to Prometheus acclaiming hope? The Prometheus festivals in Greece always honored him for the gift of fire. Obviously the survival skills made life comfortable, and their development made for the eventual spread of Greek civilization. Superior advances in technology—ships, armor, construction—made possible Hellenic supremacy throughout the Mediterranean world.

But did Prometheus see all this and wonder? Had his long waiting and observing sharpened his foresight so that he might question his own impulsive largess and his overestimation of man's ability to use his gifts wisely? Could fire ever be a wise and safe gift in the hands of ruthlessly violent humans bent on domination of neighbors and the earth itself? Perhaps Zeus' sense of human threat was not exaggerated; perhaps he sensed more clearly than Prometheus that humankind was not yet ready for fire. Humans had not adequately learned how to live together in harmonious relationship, with empathy and compassion. One of their most troublesome traits was their consistent tendency toward competitiveness. They were not prepared for fire and the lethal inventions such an energy potential could engender.

Could Prometheus see, even a few centuries ahead, what would happen to this great Greek civilization —how the greed, the ambition to conquer and master, in fact the whole heroic stance of its citizens, would lead to destruction? Where were long-range planning, democracy inclusive of all women and men, arbitration, discussion, education, an end to slavery, justice for all? Self-satisfaction and complacency, which can follow individual achievement, were numbing and stultifying the development of the social order.

In the last sentence of *Prometheus Bound*, Prometheus calls out to his mother, Themis:

> O Holy mother mine,
> O Sky that circling brings the light to all,
> you see me, how I suffer, how unjustly.[11]

The play ends with the noise and destruction of Zeus' thunderbolt. Hermes, Prometheus, and the great rock disappear. The stage is empty.

The quiet, massive audience remains silent and apprehensive. The second and third sections of the trilogy are still to follow—although these parts are lost to us, who can, moreover, only be present at the theater in our imaginations. The performance may last until nightfall. This is a solemn, ritualistic event, not to be hurried, not to be taken lightly. Greek myths, we must remind ourselves, are not fairy tales—there are no lived-happily-ever-after endings. Such endings are for children who face a long future and should not be deprived of trust and hope to grow on. Reality is more often grim than gay. In the Athenian theater one faced reality, the truth!

The grim truth, for the fifth-century-B.C. audience then present, was that history was in the process of preparing unthinkable developments. Within fifty years Athens would be utterly defeated by Sparta, the city plundered and devastated. After the breach of the impregnable walls and the destruction of the sacred olive trees by vengeful neighbors, even the Acropolis and temples would be in rubble. History makes its claim:

431 B.C.	Beginning of the Peloponnesian War
404	Athens destroyed by Sparta
371	Sparta defeated by Thebes
362	Thebes collapses; Athens rises again to power
338	King Philip II of Macedon defeats Athens
336	Philip II assassinated; Alexander succeeds
323	Alexander dies, successors carve up empire
264	Beginning of First Punic War
218	Beginning of Second Punic War
149	Rome takes over most of Greece

What are the costs of such lack of foresight? What happens to the earth? Trees in the countryside are cut down, wooded hills laid bare—erosion follows. Country folk huddle into cities for protection and profit, losing their autonomy and the former employment of their husbandry skills. More import from other lands is mandatory as local earth resources become depleted. The gap between the rich and poor grows and industry is inadequate in its support of the army and navy. The earth is laid waste and polluted by the careless exploitation of war and domination.

Perhaps Prometheus was able to foresee these on-coming catastrophes. In his enfeebled state, even with the help of the great hero Heracles, what could he have done?

Aeschylus' golden quill has long since been lost. But myth-making belongs to us all! Myths endure by being changed; they change with the times that prevail and bend to the current need of those that look to them for clarity, truth, and guidance. So now let us proceed to contemporary myth-making and a modern version of "Prometheus *Unbound*."

Prometheus Unbound

Persons in the Action

Heracles
Prometheus
Zeus
Athena
Peitho

Chorus of the Six Senses, Hope and Enlightenment:

Videra	Contacto
Savoro	(Kines) Thesia
Audera	Espera (Blue)
Scentoro	Lumino (Gold)

Scene I

The topmost crag of the Caucasus. There is almost no light. Prometheus hangs nailed to the rockface by a wedge through his torso, hands and feet chained, his head drooping. Along the base of a lower crag, in rock-like shades, the backs of the sleeping Chorus appear like layers of scree off the ledges. When the Chorus turn, their gowns display a spectrum of colors.

Throughout, each Chorus member hums one personal note consistently—sometimes muted, sometimes loud, sometimes a moan, depending on the action.

Soft gray-blue light increases.

Espera rises slowly, moves front-stage, and greets the dawning light. She looks down and follows an advancing speck in the distance. She wakens Videra, who in turn wakens Lumino. Friezelike, they read the approach of whatever is coming. The rest of the Chorus awake slowly and in silent excitement join them.

Very stealthily, Heracles sidles in from the still-shadowy left forestage, bow in hand, scanning the horizon and sky. The Chorus follow his gaze and see the approaching vulture. The Chorus return to their original positions against the rock face. Heracles leaps center-stage and shoots at the sky. There is a sound of massive weight falling; the vulture crashes down. The stage floods with daybreak. The Chorus rise, turning toward Prometheus, gilded with light. Their humming strengthens and rises.

Prometheus opens his eyes with difficulty. He wearily tries to move his head, sees the vulture, tries again to focus. Amazed at the vulture's death, he takes in the scene until his eyes fix in wonder on Heracles. Videra, Lumino, and Thesia hum loud and strong.

PROMETHEUS
Hhhh . . . Heerrr . . . Heracles!

(*Entire Chorus hum with excitement. Heracles stands immo-bilized, slowly raises hands in awed salutation.*)

Son of Zeus—you have come.

(*Spoken slowly—every breath and word an incredible effort—head sinks again.*)

HERACLES
(*Moves slowly forward—drops his bow—raises Prometheus' head in his cupped hands. Contacto loud.*)

No words, Prometheus, until your chains are loosed.
Trust me.

(*Kneels at Prometheus' feet.*)

First the feet—sturdy because they have borne
Your weight—bone-thin as they are.
The chains are almost rusted out.
Let me rub and bend your knees
So you may sense your coming freedom.

(*The Chorus moan in sympathy—loud notes from Thesia and Contacto. Prometheus makes sounds of pained appreciation—half moaning. Heracles stands.*)

Now this right arm—no old chains
Can hold against my anger.

(*Frees right hand.*)

Let me place this hand high on my shoulder.
The left one now—how light it is,
How stiff from waiting—
Let it too rest on my shoulder as it can.
Now I must withdraw the wedge,
Driven through you deep into the stone,
This is the cruelest one of all.

I can bear your whole weight—
I am supporting you . . . There, it is done.
Come, prop yourself against this rock.
Here, there is a patch of earth,
A bit of green and fragrant grass.

PROMETHEUS
Heracles . . . you are here—and I can touch, reclaim
This body so close and yet so foreign to me.
My fingertips are dull and stiff
Yet filled with want and wonder.

HERACLES
(*From a fissure in the rock, Heracles catches water in his cupped hands to bring to Prometheus' lips.*)

Come drink, another sensation
For your wasted body.

(*Heracles sits on his heels at Prometheus' feet.*)

When you can, tell me how you have borne
This eternity of waiting, what thoughts
Have occupied your mind
Sustained you and your purpose
You hero of unflagging hope.

PROMETHEUS
I have had much time for thought.
How shall I find words and voice to tell you?

(*Slowly and with great feeling*)

Immobilized against bare rock, the pain
Always gnawing at me—yet my feet
On the ground bonded me with my great mother.
With mist, wind, and earthbound sense,
She managed to sustain me.
Her snake coiled round my feet at night,
Guarded and strengthened me.

Snakes, allied with earth forces
Kept my knees from cracking.

HERACLES
Slowly Prometheus, slowly. We have time.

PROMETHEUS
(*Slow crescendo of Chorus*)

In the desolate aloneness as my muscles
Slowly numbed, my senses seemed to sharpen;
I grew aware of all surrounding me.
Sun, rain, and wind were friend as well as foe,
Active and enlivening, they brought change
And kept me from despair. I came to be at one
With little crawling, flying creatures,
Soon I did not mind their small bites;
My skin toughened.
They bore me no malice—they were just hungry.
They live together, I saw, in surprising harmony,
Sharing the earth and sky, busy with living.

CHORUS
(*On their own notes*)
He speaks of skills unknown to men,
The arts of peace and harmony.
Such words hold wisdom for this hero
Who listens only with one ear.
Though has he not come here to learn?

PROMETHEUS
Oh, more water, Heracles—how the slippery
Coolness moistens my tongue and throat.

Slowly I reviewed my life—
Those years of hopeful planning.
I recalled every word and mood
Of the first days on this rock—

The conversations with my visitors;
I marveled at how words and talk had helped me.
When Oceanus said, "Words are healers of wrath"
I scoffed, but that proved true for me.
His daughters urged, "Tell us your story,"
And I found great comfort in the telling.
Io had so pled with me to share my foresight
Of her future, that I revealed more than intended.
That too brought release from the tension
Of my outrage, a kind of healing followed.
Language is a binding link,
Bridging past, present, and future.
I pondered how this tool could better
Serve us all in the art of living.
I myself gave mortals speech and reason,
But only Peitho knows persuasion.

HERACLES
Words have never served me thus—
I have no time for chatter.
What you say does not convince me.
Deeds and action are called for
No time wasted on mere talk.

PROMETHEUS
In time I saw with hindsight
What should have been foreseen.
Acting as I did, I deserved what I got.
I could even see that my deviousness
In stealing fire as a gift to men
Had created the breech with Zeus
And could in the long run have been a mistake.
Zeus saw more than I did;
I have serious premonitions. . . .

I reviewed my cause against
This god, originally my partner.

My low regard for his dull wits
Enraged that insecure tyrant.
Words not acts might have been more winning.
To rebel against Zeus was pure hubris.
I searched my mind for a method
To oppose without being abrasive.
Only persuasion can bring about change;
Peitho's agents are tone, voice, and language.

CHORUS
(*Chant, on their own notes*)
Prometheus grows tired—unused as he is to speech.
Heracles listens, puzzled and silent.
The impulsive one, Prometheus, has changed.
With time and great suffering, he has grown wiser.

PROMETHEUS
Water again would refresh me, Heracles.
Lift my head and shoulder.
Ah . . . your strong hands pour life into me.
Ah this water! It tastes as fresh grass smells
And gleams like diamonds melting—
My mother earth has sent it
From depths of the darkened river
A force that spurs and fosters life
And feeds the waving grain of Attica.

But still I falter—tell me, Heracles,
Of those great deeds that made you
The world's own hero.

HERACLES
I will and gladly. I was so young then
And inflated with my strength.
Fifty days it took, to hunt the Cithaeron lion
Who ravaged the mighty herds
Of Thespius, King of Thespiae,
Though the nights with his daughters were restful!

I needed all my training, a magnificent beast he was.
We matched our skills and powers.
I was single-minded, fought with the zest of youth
In the final conflict—fought and conquered. . . .

CHORUS
A well-fought fight—a splendid victory,
You, great hero, came back with the hide,
Wearing the beast's gaping head: a well-won trophy.
The gods smiled. All Hellas hailed your heroism.

PROMETHEUS
Ah yes—all people sang your praises;
Then you went on to kill the Nemean lion,
The Lernaean hydra, and the Stymphalian birds.
(*Pause*)
What if you'd just trapped this game—
Built enclosures to surround them?
Willing hands would have helped you.
Trapped and safe, all would have come
To marvel at these great creatures
Until they lived their lives out.
They were unique but not immortal—
Their like will never again be seen.

Heracles, you had no need to kill the vulture
So impulsively as you came here,
Grateful as I am for your coming.
Just freeing me would have been enough.
Seeing me move would have sent him flying;
He eats only carrion—no doubt thought me dead.

HERACLES
(*After a long pause*)
You don't even bear him a grudge?
(*Pause*)
But tell me, Prometheus, what does a man,
A man such as I in my youth—

What does he do with a well-trained body—
With that restless, surging energy?

PROMETHEUS
Indeed you were the living image of young hero.
No doubt you were well taught, too well perhaps,
By famous teachers in the martial skills.
But is that body not an instrument at your disposal
For many skills—other than killing?
What about music, dance . . . any of the arts?
Rumor says you killed Orpheus' brother Linus
When he tried to teach you how to play the lyre.
Did he point out some flaw in your sense of rhythm?
Is that what angered you? Can you not sing well?
Singing is one of the modes of persuasion;
Voice, a body skill, demands trained breathing.
You are and were the best—but only in violence.

HERACLES
But how can you make people change
Without the use of force?
I still do not see, Prometheus—
What choice is there but violence?

PROMETHEUS
Only non-violence.

HERACLES
Non what?

PROMETHEUS
Non-violence.

HERACLES
You suggest to *me* base cowardice, sluggish apathy?

PROMETHEUS
No, by the gods. Non-violence
May sound like mere inaction

But in truth means non-violent *action*.
I'll say again what I've come to learn:
The wisest resource against tyranny of force
Is the skill of the high goddess Peitho;
The effective means for solving dispute
Is persuasion in all her aspects:
In language, rhetoric, the sciences of nature,
In theater, discourse, and poetry—
All the arts are graced with her gift to move.

Persuasion is not a one-time gift.
To be given, as I gave fire.
It comes with learning, is an ever-growing skill
Which develops with experience over time.
Heracles, there is still much for you to master.

HERACLES
Tell us, Prometheus, who is this Peitho
Of whom you speak so reverently?
Where can I find and learn from her
These skills you prize so highly?

PROMETHEUS
She is the daughter of Ares and Aphrodite,
Drawn to each other as opposites attract.
Strong and courageous, she reaches toward love
With a yearning for mutuality.
You will surely be drawn to her, Heracles;
She knows the skills of peace.

HERACLES
But Prometheus, gods rarely speak directly to us—
I need human teachers, mentors, models.
How shall I seek them out, where find them?

PROMETHEUS
Such wise ones won't serve your purpose.
But Peitho, like Love, is spirit,

Like a muse she will whisper to guide you.
But you must pay attention, the price is high,
To win her demands a consistent response
From every fiber of your being.
Peace and harmony come slowly in life,
Need constant reaffirmation.
Living is truly a challenge.

Glorious sunrises, sunsets, moonglow
Offer respites of love, refresh the spirit.
You will recognize your comrades in the struggle,
Step in the footprints of the wisest ones
Who wear serenity like a garment.

HERACLES
But Prometheus, how do I go about all this?
I'm getting older—still, I will live on a long time.

PROMETHEUS
Yes, indefinitely long, Zeus will see to it,
And that leaves you much time to learn.
Peitho herself will guide you. Seek her out.
Call on her for support, inspiration—
She is lovely, quite irresistible.
Peitho, when the cause is worthy,
Can embody the brave stance of Ares
Or shine with Aphrodite's grace and charm.

Seek out Peitho and learn her skills.
She of the gods is most human—
Her nature is more earth-related
Than that of other Olympic dwellers.
She is more like you and me with our spectrum
Of capacities: from base to caring action.
Guided by her empathy, she knows well
The good and the beautiful,
But slyness and violence as well.

She knows well that to be human
Means to cope with conflicting urges.

CHORUS
Prometheus confronts us with ambiguities,
Challenges our feeble efforts at self-knowledge.
Will the wise one ever come with a mirror
To penetrate the masks that defend us
From seeing ourselves and the paradox
Of our true nature with which we struggle?

PROMETHEUS
You have heard it said—perhaps said it yourself—
"In war and in love all things are fair."
In truth: deceit and devious plot
Corrupt and thwart relations,
Which only endure with honesty.
Peitho knows these vital truths—
False "fairness" breeds destruction.

Zeus' contempt for creatures of a day
Breeds relationships based only on fear.
His rule, though now less vindictive,
Is still erratic, and witlessly erotic.
The time for change is now—
Change is in fact our only hope.

CHORUS
Fearless soul—once more he challenges Zeus.
What is the source of such bold courage?
What vision does his foresight offer
That prompts him to speak to Zeus' son
In this blunt and forthright manner?

HERACLES
Prometheus, you speak in such prophetic words.
What did your years of solitude reveal?

What have you foreseen that gives
Your words such urgency?

PROMETHEUS
Indeed, step by step disaster approaches.

HERACLES
Tell us, reveal everything—
We listen with foreboding.

PROMETHEUS
Let the Chorus speak for me—
I tire and they know all my premonitions.

CHORUS
He has indeed described to us how,
Looking down from this lofty crag,
He first saw lovely Hellas
Set in her sparkling waters—
Verdant and lush with living
Trees, streams, villages abounding,
All open, welcoming to neighbors—
And one lovely city more gracious
Than all others, fair-columned Athens.
But even as he looked, dark clouds gathered
Shutting out the bright rays of Apollo.

At a later time, through a cloud-free sky,
He again saw the same fair country
Now newly despoiled of much verdure:
With fortresses, walls and marked boundaries,
Oared ships or full-sailed plying the waters,
Cities a turmoil of action and building,
Weapons, cavalry, columned men marching,
Towns in ferment, no laughter or singing,

Men endlessly threatening each other,
Seeking safety in pacts and with treaties;
Controlling sea routes and small island strongholds,

Hungry for wealth, no end to their grasping
For power, complete domination—
They press on to ever new holdings
But gain only hatred, death, reprisal.

Battles grow ever more massive,
Armies move in devastating numbers,
Ships ram one another in harbors—
Shrieks, clashing weapons and armor,
Dead bodies afloat in waters
Dyed scarlet with blood of warriors—

Proud Athens, city of temples,
Of men wiser than many, but helpless
To stem the ambitions of heroes,
Wielders of power whose sole thrust
Is to dominate land, sea, and others
As if to ensure freedom forever!

Athens' walls are breached and flattened,
Sacred olive trees hacked down in hatred.
The lovely city in rubble, a waste land.
Only wailing and moans reach the heavens.

(*A deep mourning sound comes from the Chorus. They move
in slow, funereal fashion—heads low and heavy-footed—
around the stage. There is a dirgelike, low drumbeat.*)

(*Pause*)

HERACLES
You have been here too long, Prometheus.
Greeks are not stupid—wise and learned men
Will safely steer the ship of state.
They speak and write well, acclaim harmony,
Frown with the gods on hubris,
And do not tolerate tyranny.

PROMETHEUS
That is true, Heracles, but ambitious statesmen,
Generals with lust for power, are also there.
When shields flash and clash,
Feet march and banners fly,
All Greece rises up to cheer and follow.
This does merchants no harm—they forge
The tools of conflict and expedition.
You yourself have seen this often;
It is bracing, all join in with fervor.

HERACLES
You malign the loyalty due to our land.
Surely the cause is always a worthy one.

PROMETHEUS
But who foresees the outcome?
Who truly counts the cost
In blood and desolation?
War breeds hate and retaliation.
To protect is instinctive—to attack,
Expand power, and dominate is reckless.

HERACLES
To me this seems natural—every state does it.
Push the edges out to safeguard the center.
Spread out, take over, and enlarge the market.

PROMETHEUS
Who says this is natural? It is the curse of mankind.
It seems natural since it's taught from infancy on.
It is lauded as manly, heroic—Greek.

HERACLES
What would you have us do?
Become effete—like women?

PROMETHEUS

Observe the women in their households:
With fortitude they endure the pangs of birthing,
How lovingly they care for children.
They know the earth forces and plants,
Act as wise healers for their families.
Their wisdom includes the virtues of foods,
And the arts of their preparation;
They spin and weave cloth that covers our bodies;
They build, repair, work tirelessly
For the good of all,
And in the family they act as peace-makers.
These are the survival skills we depend on.
Women are needed in the councils
Of the leaders and the decision-makers.

CHORUS

These are wise words he gives voice to.
But should he speak thus in Athens
He would be stoned or laughed to scorn.
Yet Athena, once goddess of the hearth,
Is Athens' goddess of wisdom.
How odd these mortals are.

HERACLES

The future you foretell,
Prometheus, is like a dirge.
How can we hope to defend our land
From this dreadful fate?
It moves in on us even as we speak.

PROMETHEUS

Words are powerful, Heracles—
Words and a few broken statues
Will be all that remains of Greece unless
We swiftly move to change this course
That flows as forcefully as a river in flood.

HERACLES
What then is to be our stategy?
Tell us. Give me action.

PROMETHEUS
All your zest and drive will be needed,
But not your violent skills. Let us plan.
As I said earlier, and you were not impressed,
You must seek out the lovely Peitho.
Don't be biased because she's a woman.
Remember, she works side by side with Athena
In all her solemn judgments.

HERACLES
Tell me more about Peitho.
Why have I heard so little of this goddess?
Too often she's derided
As Aphrodite's tricky accomplice.

PROMETHEUS
Heracles—do you remember the madness of Orestes
When those earth forces, the Furies,
Viciously hounded him for slaying his own mother?
Nothing could satisfy their thirst for revenge.
Even Athena was baffled.

Then Peitho came to the rescue, whispered
A peaceful solution into the ear of the goddess:
"Don't be biased, gracious Athena.
These old Furies are clearly justified.
In a world of hungry animals,
To which all humans belong,
The helpless young are the choicest,
Most prized and succulent prey—
Lamb, calf, suckling pig, infant—
Mothers risk their lives for their offspring,
For the young they've brought into this world.
To kill your own mother is indeed a heinous sin.

These Furies through the ages have pursued
Such grave offenders, making their lives a misery.
Orestes is such a one. In a world of heroes,
Values too often become distorted.
Reframe your charge, Athena.
Offer the Furies a new role. Make them guardians
Of Athens, win them over with new honors.
Let their power serve peace, not retribution.
All Athens will rejoice and make merry.

Thus it was done, the rejoicing was genuine,
Added fame and luster to Athena—and Athens.
But the solution was Peitho's;
Peitho the peace-maker.

For the polis she is essential—
When problems are negotiated with open
And rational argument, she is present.
She soothes away anger in the voices
Of the lawyer, the doctor, the citizen.
Most movingly, her voice is resonant
In the theater, our revered temple of learning.

HERACLES
I am silenced—I had not understood
Her role or her great power.

CHORUS
How eloquently he speaks,
Prometheus the obdurate one.
Indeed the weary years have changed him;
Can he persuade Heracles, the model hero?

HERACLES
I am drawn to this lady, this goddess.
Force and Might have served me well
But certain graces have been lacking.
Where shall I find Peitho, how join her?
You clever one, Prometheus—you have a plan.

PROMETHEUS
You will know well how to propitiate Peitho.
She does not hide but waits to be called.
Her eyes will charm you, lend you power
And conviction. This is my plan:
You two will join forces and go to Olympus.
There tell the gods all I have foreseen for Hellas.
They will be stunned, for this future
Would leave them lords over rubble, a poor show.
You will win their attention and collaboration.

CHORUS
He plans with bold, far-reaching strokes
This friend of humankind.
He sees their imperfections
And their thoughtless plunge toward doom.
But his pity for their humanness
Gnaws at him, like the vulture.
His hope, the hope that Themis gave,
Sustains and binds him to his purpose
And his love of earthly things.

PROMETHEUS
The time is now and, as always, flying past us.

I shall not go with you to Olympus—
Indeed that would be foolish.
When Zeus is ready he will seek me out.
Take me, Heracles, to a verdant edge of the sea.
There Poseidon and his daughters will help me
And earth forces heal my weakened body.
You will find me there if you need me.
Be hopeful—we are late and all change is slow.
We may fail to alter the course of history,
Humans and gods are slow to change their ways.
But somewhere there must be a beginning,
One that you and Peitho alone can foster.

CHORUS

There by the pulse of the wine-dark sea
We will make a shrine in reverence to Peitho:
Fragrant blossoms will sweeten the air,
Soft mosses caress weary feet,
Honeyed berries bend thornless branches,
Brilliant butterflies drift through the air,
And playful waves toss shoreward
A tribute of golden shells.

With all this your great mother will help us—
For it is only through persuasive fullness
That the earth herself is productive.
There you will heal and there Peitho
Will respond to your earnest call—
Nothing could be more persuasive
Than your proud suffering, Prometheus.

(*Lights dim somewhat as Prometheus and Heracles slowly leave stage-right with Chorus. As they leave, eight new Chorus members quietly enter from backstage. Backing up against the rocky crag (four on each side), they slowly push the stones back and sideward to create a large space between the stones. The original eight Chorus members then reenter and join the new members in a circle, each one facing a partner. They move mechanically forward around the circle like the ticking of a clock. As curtain rises behind the rocks to reveal an icy bluish and misty Olympus, the Chorus back up in a curved line, eight on each side.*)

Scene II

(*Heracles and Peitho enter. They look around with curiosity.
Humming of the Chorus continues throughout—sometimes intoned as questions and answers, sometimes surprise, apprehension, etc.*)

CHORUS

Heracles and Peitho have revealed
The prophecy of disaster to Olympus,
Have spoken in their theater
To the assembled gods and goddesses.
There is a grave silence in the air.
Zeus' eyes flash with anger.

ZEUS

(*Voice heard from behind audience. Lights flash. All onstage
turn to face the voice.*)

Heracles, earthborn son, you are here because
Peitho, hard to resist, begged to bring you.
Prometheus, that stubborn Titan,
I would not have admitted. How craftily
He has sent you with this disaster story.
He overstates the hazards, of course—
I'm not surprised. Yet, humans do consistently
Tend to fall prey to hubris—
All those ships, their boundless greed—
They overstep their limits.
A flawed race. But speak, what is your errand?

HERACLES

Father Zeus, you have been my support,
Found me skilled teachers—I am grateful.
But I've been impetuous, hot-tempered, and rash,
And for killing served others as penalty.
I have had no set purpose to guide my own life.

Now, with Peitho, I would try to steer men
On another course than that foretold.
Peitho has been your daughter Athena's ally;
Now she will also be mine. Give us your blessing.

ZEUS
I have no reason to resist you, Peitho.
What you accomplish is always surprising.
But I have some northern snowcapped mountains
To reshape and other important business.
I must be on my way.

(*There is a long silence—almost a sigh of relief. Heracles and
Peitho look at one another questioningly. Athena slowly appears
from the wings. Heracles greets Athena with reverence; Peitho's
greeting to Athena is more intimate. Athena faces the cast.*)

ATHENA
I have been goddess of the hearth
In those lands that border the great waters—
In Hellas, clothed in armor,
I became protector of Athens.
Over the years she grew into
A city of beauty and veneration for gods,
But you know well, as I do,
That things are clearly changing:
Sharp minds have now been honing,
Groping for new understanding
Of the universe and its nature.
The wisdom I have nurtured
Has brought me keener foresight,
A skill so precious to survival.
I sense great change surging forward.
"Thoughts and Ideas, the fair
And immortal children of the mind,"
Have found voice and are maturing
Increasing their power, their influence,
To excite many scholars and thinkers.

We gods are still loved for our beauty
But our control of mortals is slipping—
Mortal minds outpace our stagnant perfection,
Will soon no longer accept our domination.

Peitho, you, as usual, are quiet until
Sought after—like a muse, speak to us.

PEITHO
What you say, Athena, is wise and true.
Mortals celebrate our festivals with pleasure,
Delighting in old forms and ceremonies,
But they convene very shortly after
To discuss new findings in science
Or something now called philosophy.
Minds are elsewhere even as they praise us.

CHORUS
(*Clinging to one another*)
These new thoughts make our mountain shiver
From a thunderbolt not thrown by Zeus.
Athena seems to grow in stature,
The wise one—Zeus' unnatural daughter
Whose owl eyes penetrate the dark,
Know when and where to strike.

ATHENA
We would be wise to abandon
Our cold mountain home. Leave Olympus,
Cease to consort and drink mead together.
We are alone—Zeus is off; we are free to consider
What our role among mortals might be—
Work that befits the events that now face us,
Face Athens—face Greece and her future.

Let us merge into the world of mortals:
With skills well known to us we can
Infuse myth and legend with our living presence,
Inhabit serene columns, activate frescoes,

Breathe life into statues, the work of all artists—
Nurture and illuminate beauty.
Thus we will not be forgotten
Living on in each precious fragment.
In our own ways we will live on
To sharpen the senses, open eyes and ears,
Invest touch, smell, taste, and dancing,
Enriching mortals and the great earth around us.

CHORUS
If the tide of history, now hard upon us,
Is too strong for us to contend with,
Let us sit at the feet of Peitho,
Learn from her the skills of persuasion.
Conflicts need words, arbitration, and time.
Threats and force cannot really solve problems.

PEITHO
We have lived long years on Olympus
Hovering over the fates of the Hellenes,
Unaging, unchanging, slowly freezing
Like bodies preserved in old glaciers.
Change supports growth itself, which is living,
Growth forces change, which results in becoming,
Time never stands still—that's stagnation.
Perfection we achieved, Excellence we've supported,
But high altitudes do not generate laughter,
Healthy "see yourself" humor is lacking.
Look at us, all such atrophied statues,
Who never experienced childhood.
Down to earth there are children to play with.
They delight in paradox; love giggles and humor,
Laughter that sets all the bells ringing.

ATHENA
Come, come now with me. Leave frigid Olympus.
Join with humans for justice and truth,
For survival, joy, beauty, and laughter.

(*The two groups of Chorus are joined by children from the audience. Much activity. As the lights begin to dim, nursery songs are played from all directions: Higglety, pigglety, pop—the mouse ran up the clock; Frère Jacques; See-saw Marjorie Daw; Wee Willie Winkie; Humpty Dumpty sat on a wall; Round and round the mulberry bush; Jack and Jill went up the hill; Three blind mice; etc. These tunes can be harmonized into a delightful blend of children's voices and tin-whistle sounds. As the theater continues to darken, members of the Chorus and perhaps some members of the audience turn flashlights on and off, or swirl them around to create an effect of flickering light, like fireflies. As the songs and light movements increase, children from the audience lead the Chorus and cast off the stage and up through the audience to the back of the theater. Stagehands follow with masks, statues, columns, chains, bow, pieces of crag, etc.*)

Orpheus

Out of the mythical, pre-Homeric past a figure slowly emerges. We first see him depicted in sculpture; he is standing with unnamed companions on the prow of a vessel. The clearly decipherable Greek letters ορφΑΣ indicate that he is Orpheus; and the vessel is the *Argo*, the ship which sailed to Colchis in search of the Golden Fleece. Who is this personage, and what is there about him that commands our attention? There is evidence that he did live on this earth, but, through the centuries, whatever may have been factual about his life has been absorbed into creative legend.

The name Orpheus is first mentioned in the sixth century B.C. by the poet Ibykos, who refers to him, even then, as "the renowned Orpheus," father of music, poetry, and prophecy. He was reputed to be the son of either Apollo, the sun god, or the river demigod Oeagrus, and Calliope, the muse of epic poetry. He seems to have been blessed at birth by all the other muses: as a poet he was credited with being the patron of all the arts, and, indeed, he augmented his lyre from seven to nine strings in order to celebrate all the nine muses. Singing and playing on his lyre, Orpheus made music so divinely that both the animate and inanimate world listened and responded with ecstasy. "The animals would all go still, the wind would lay limp in the grass so's not to blow away one note of that sweet music."[1] Or, as Shakespeare has it, "And Orpheus with his lute made trees / And the mountain tops that freeze / Bow themselves when he did sing." The soft tones of the lyre provided an appropriate accompaniment instrument for the melodic mode with which he established the lyrical tradition as distinguished from the wild and sometimes frenzied music of the Dionysian rites—the Bacchanalia.

There is little recorded in the early Greek myths and legends about music, song, and dance except as elements of religious ceremony. Drumming in a martial manner is suggested, as is the clashing of cymbals; poetry is rhythmic, but of singing perhaps only the sirens come to mind. In the Argonaut story, music is mentioned as a poisonous trap used by the sirens, a lure to be feared and avoided, a deceptive soporific. However, vase paintings and sculpture are tantalizingly suggestive of dance, piping, and song. It is hard to imagine that these arts were not a rich element in Greek life. Perhaps poetry was half sung with a strummed accompaniment. Calliope, the muse of epic poetry, is alluded to as "she of the beautiful voice." Perhaps she sang lullabies to the infant Orpheus. In all portrayals of this "born musician" we recognize him by his lyre. Orpheus consistently sang; there is no suggestion that he ever merely spoke, but if he did, it was surely poetry.

Orpheus made use of his musical mastery while

Orpheus with his lyre.

sailing with Jason and the Argonauts in search of the Golden Fleece. The Golden Fleece was the hide of a flying ram which carried Phrixus to safety when he was about to be sacrificed by his father, Athamas, ruler of Thebes. Phrixus sacrificed the ram to Zeus and gave its fleece of pure gold to Aeetes, ruler of Colchis. It was hung from an oak tree in a shrine dedicated to Ares, god of war. Guarded by a serpent and magic powers, it was Colchis' greatest treasure.

Born in the city of Iolcus, Jason, the son of Aeson, was under the protection of the goddess Hera and raised by the centaur Chiron on Mount Pelion. King Pelias, the younger brother of Aeson, was uneasy about his claim to the throne. When an oracle warned him of impending misfortune, he sent Jason off on a dangerous trip to Colchis to claim the Golden Fleece, which was kept under constant guard. He ordered ships to be built and sent out a proclamation throughout Greece for aspiring heroes to join the crew.

The list of heroes joining in this adventure is awesome, each one a master of a particular skill; even Heracles and Atalanta were among them, and Peleus, the father of Achilles. At Chiron's counsel, Orpheus was urged to join the expedition in order to keep the oarsmen in rhythm by the pulse of his music and, also with his music, to protect the crew from the enchantment of the sirens, whose singing was known to lure sailors to their destruction. Naturally there was much quarreling among the aspiring heroes in the crew of the *Argo*, and one of Orpheus' roles was to dispel their anger with his music and his songs about the beauty of the world and the greatness and goodness of the gods.

On the day of their departure they were unable to launch the *Argo*, their great ship. Orpheus was called upon to encourage them with his lyre, whereupon *Argo* launched herself, a feat that awed the participants as well as the onlookers. He later charmed the Clashing Rocks so that the *Argo* could pass between them safely. And when they finally reached Colchis and drew near the serpent that guarded the fleece, he sang so enchantingly that the great beast slept. The details of these stories we learn from the Orphic *Argonautica* and the *Argonautica* of Apollonius Rhodius.

What else did the wise old centaur Chiron expect Orpheus to provide for the Argonauts? To succeed, to win the day at all costs, was the heroic stance, but this was also dangerous, for the Olympian gods were supreme and allowed unaided human success only up to a point. The gods demanded to be included and propitiated appropriately. If this was ignored—this gesture of proper humility—the hero might be found guilty of hubris, of excessive and presumptuous pride. The older vintage of mortals knew this well; the young and eager learned it only under wise counsel or through unfortunate experience.

Thus Orpheus took a leadership role in all religious matters: he performed the inaugural sacrifice before departure, he encouraged the Argonauts to become initiated into the mysteries at Samothrace, and he sacrificed to atone for accidental killings. Purification rites were performed at Malea, and sacrifices dedicated to the rulers of the underworld were made just before the victorious return of the *Argo*. There are further accounts of Orpheus' leadership. His prayers to the gods of mariners saved the ship from a storm because he had been initiated into their mysteries. He persuaded the crew to offer the tripod of Apollo to the gods to ensure a safe return, and composed the appropriate hymn when Jason dedicated the *Argo* at Corinth. Surely these are priestly functions and suggest his later involvement with what are known as the Orphic mysteries. Apollonius records that the songs Orpheus sang to calm the quarrels of the sailors were also of a religious nature—about the origin of life and all things, and the birth of the gods—hymns that evoke something other than the strident rhythms of sailors' chanties. The Orphic *Argonautica* notes that this was also the quality of his song in the home of Chiron, the centaur. Such are the stories pieced together from fragments accrued by writers in later epochs.[2]

The statements you have read so far about Orpheus in this essay or in any other are debatable. There was no student like Plato, no constant admirer such as Boswell, to record Orpheus' life and views. Yet the name and the lyre remain constant in all reports and in all the images on artifacts—pots, mirrors, gemstones—which have been preserved over the centuries. In some form he existed, and he continues to command a place in our imaginations. For hundreds of years human beings have been grateful to him for unnamed gifts, blessings which have been sensed rather than made explicit. Given the uncertainty of his actual historicity, there have been those who scoffed and challenged his very existence. However, the power of myths and legends does not lie in making a sharp intellectual point, but rather in an appeal to shared values presented in memorable form. Myths may be considered on many levels, depending on the maturity and curiosity of the reader, the attention of the listener.

At the heart of the Orpheus legend is the account of the loss of his beloved wife, Eurydice, who dies of a snakebite and descends into the underworld. Orpheus determines to pursue her there and bring her back to the land of the living. He undertakes a journey involving awesome obstacles. First he encounters Cerberus, the fierce, three-headed dog who guards the gates of hell. But when he plays his lyre, Cerberus is tamed and allows Orpheus to enter the underworld. Once there, he succeeds in gaining passage over the river Styx, ferried by Charon, who is charmed by the power of his song. His greatest challenge, of course, is to convince Hades himself, the ruler of the underworld, to grant the release of Eurydice. The song Orpheus then plays and sings is so poignant that Persephone, the wife of Hades, is reduced to tears and Hades gives his assent. But there is one condition: Orpheus may neither touch nor look back at Eurydice until they both set foot into the light of the sun. Orpheus leads Eurydice up through the darkness with his song and the music of his lyre, but as he first moves into the light, he turns to look at her and perhaps to reach back for her before she has stepped into the sunlight—in so doing, he loses her forever.

This is the famous myth, beloved of storytellers, poets, composers, and natural scientists, as told and retold in great detail throughout the centuries. Why does it charm and somehow challenge all those who have responded to it and tried to give it new dimensions? Woven, embroidered, sculptured in marble, cast in bronze, painted on canvas, sung in opera,

acted in drama, celebrated in poetry, and danced—
it must have been danced. Even this chantlike listing
may change one's mood and rhythm. It is the age-
old tale of loving, having, losing, longing, and the
superhuman effort to regain, finally thwarted by repeated failure. It is blatantly the story of one man—
every man—Orpheus. Eurydice is the victim of the
snakebite, but is otherwise only presented as the
object of loving desire. Her wish is in no way
elicited—does she have one? Persephone, in her
turn, only weeps; that is her language, the language
of loss too deep for words.

There are other aspects of this trip down into the
underworld that grip and hold us. Isn't Hades where
we all sink down to when overwhelming loss ob-
scures the sun and we are out of touch, deprived
of the energy and light that give life meaning? It
is a lonesome way—black, cold, barren. However,
some of the most beautiful substances the earth has
produced are embedded in those mine-deep rocks—
alabaster, rubies, lapis lazuli, and veins of gold and
silver. The artist's eye, which has become aware and
open, may bring with it glimmers of light, enough
to see and be startled by such beauty, unexpected
and enlivening.

As all healers know, and infants through the ages
have learned early, soft singing, even moaning, may
help to ease aloneness. Sound is comforting and especially so when sight fails. What could Orpheus
have sung on his way down to give himself courage
and to win the necessary sanction of the guards to
his passing? Surely his song was of love and yearning, for we assume these filled his heart. And to what

music would Eurydice have responded, in that strange world of shades, to lure her up the steep way to light and verdure? The lively sounds of earth would naturally catch her ear in that dull space: bird songs at dawn; wind rustling trees; gurgling of streams; animal sounds—braying, barking, even the buzz of bees; perhaps an old familiar lullaby or alluring rhyme songs from her childhood. We may assume that she was starving for such sounds in Hades.

Loss, then, is the theme—the futility of any effort to recapture. Acceptance and the challenge of facing loss creatively are made memorable and tangible for all mortals. We are left with one puzzle: why did Orpheus look back? His task was to sing and play to Eurydice all the way into Apollo's domain. In prematurely turning back, he no doubt released his hand from the lyre and interrupted the flow of song too soon—the task uncompleted, the work unfinished. For the artist a failure? Failure, any failure or falling down on an assignment, is essentially painful and upsetting in many ways beyond that of physical injury. Basic trust in your own trustworthiness, autonomy, initiative, competence, and identity are all denigrated and challenged. These are the very building blocks of self-respect and stand in need of fundamental repair. A really watertight excuse or someone to take on some part of the blame is a godsend, though these backups never quite leave you standing tall. For the artist, however, a failure is only one lost opportunity, not final, not the end. As an artist, Orpheus never stopped singing of his love as well as of his loss, sharing with the animate and even inanimate world his praise and his longing. He transformed his failure and his loss into a legacy for all who fail and lose.

Another aspect of this "failure" interests me. The decision as to whether Orpheus' father was the great Apollo or Oeagrus is left open for us. The choice of the lyre as his instrument and emblem links him to Apollo, who also played the lyre. But Apollo's son would have been immortal. Oeagrus was only a demigod and was more human, like Orpheus. It moves me to think that Orpheus' very humanness was expressed in this small but heartbreaking misstep. He had made a perilous journey, overcome grave obstacles, and succeeded marvelously, and he was yearning for the reward, to actually see, perhaps touch, Eurydice. How human, how understandable and endearing. Or perhaps one should be reminded of a small boy venturing across an open space like an empty kitchen floor, who stops suddenly in his tracks to look back, to check for reassurance that the parent and safety are still there—that very human moment of self-doubt, of need for approval or another gulp of courage, yearned for by that child within us all. In any case, we are persuaded that a staunch heroic character would, of course, have stalwartly won through to the goal. How we admire such firm single-mindedness; but Orpheus is one of us and our hearts go out to him.

Sonnets to Orpheus
II
13

Be ahead of all parting, as though it were behind
you, like the winter that is even now leaving.
For under winters one is so endlessly winter,
that, winter spent, your heart fully revives.

Be forever dead in Eurydice—climb singing,
climb back praising into the clear connectedness.
Here, among the waning ones, be, in the realm of shades,
be—a ringing glass, that shatters itself in the ringing.

Be—and at the same time know the way of nonbeing,
the infinite ground of your inner resonance,
which this one time you may wholly fulfill.

To the useful as to the muffled and the mute
of nature's full store, those immeasurable sums,
count yourself in, rejoicing, and cancel the cost.

R.M. RILKE
TR. J.M.E.

An amazing harvest of artistic energy was generated by ancient Greece, and I shall claim Orpheus as its progenitor and guiding spirit. Orpheus evoked a groundswell of creative endeavor, glorying in the beauty of the world and the capacity of human beings to be productive and creative in their lives. What a panacea the arts offer humankind! Loss is constant and inevitable, Orpheus seemed to be singing. How can anything be made permanent except through immortalizing it in created form? The dragonfly flits by—observe it, appreciate, rejoice in its beauty, and perhaps record it in plastic form, in color, in dance, in memory and song. Orpheus' voice is still compelling. Creativity is our greatest asset, our hope-filled strength. Without it we live as beggars on a dull earth.

Perhaps what distinguishes mortals most from the gods is that mortals are losers: we *have*, but for the moment only. The moment passes, and all that remains is a possible change in us and a memory, which fades and dims in time if not caught, given substance, and made somewhat permanent. But there is joy in that moment and in the essence of life itself. For the ever-young Greek gods, time was endless and they themselves unchanging. This sameness must have been really quite boring today, tomorrow, and forever. With no court jester in their midst, they no doubt reveled in human clowns—did they sense enough about paradox to yield to the joy and release of humor? They all took themselves very seriously and insisted on due respect from humankind and one another. One could begin to feel sorry for those permanently constrained to live a laughterless life on Mount Olympus. But human affairs, as they perceived them from the heights, must have provided them with an entertaining spectacle, like a great dramatic production in a massive outdoor amphitheater. They could select favorite players, float down from their lofty appointed seats, whisper in an actor's ears, nudge adroitly and change the direction of the action. If the outcome of this prod caused the actor to do something drastically immoral or unjust, the earth forces, the Eumenides, could and would vigorously accuse and threaten punishment. But the human actor could then still plead that a god had inspired or conjured the act.

Of course, we all establish our own myths, blaming our genes, predispositions, and parents for our behavior, especially when it is questionable. Childhood can be nightmare or fairy tale. We selectively remember what fits into our personal myth—the remainder, good or bad, is dismissed as irrelevant. Vested in our social identities we face the world. We create our myths, justifying our lives in order to avoid our own meaninglessness. Perhaps these personal myths help to support one's invariable core, which is not blown with the winds of change and chance. We demand of ourselves the appropriate "living out" of our own myths, with inner consistency. This programmed enterprise becomes an ongoing challenge to lethargy and the unavoidable trials of aging.

We mortals truly have only the moment to live in—from moment to moment. Constantly at the helm of our own ship, sound or in poor shape, we must steer and be alone responsible for our own course—light or dark, cloudy or clear, guided by the stars we elect to steer by. And time ticks past with every heartbeat, faster and faster as the years pass. This is the script for all sentient beings. The wise accept their allotted role and the players with whom they share the stage; they try to learn to make each moment count by attending to the richness of relationships, to the beauty of the set, and by paying close attention to the amazing and wonderful detail of all created things.

Orpheus was, I believe, trying to sing us into understanding, and thus into accepting and affirming our space of life. The way he offers us is to join him in song in whatever way song comes most truly—sadly, with joy, loud or soft, for ourselves or for others. Song is never out of place, for it embraces all ranges of human feeling, from a banshee's wailing warning to hilarious drinking songs, from low mourning to soft crooning and the tenderest love lyric.

Sonnets to Orpheus
I
7

Praising is all! Praise was his mission,
and he came forth as ore comes, from the rock's
silence. His heart, an ephemeral winepress
of inexhaustible wine for mankind.

In the dust his voice never fails him
once the godhead has him in its grip.
Everything becomes vineyard, all things turn grape
ripened in his sensuous South.

No mold in the royal burial vault,
nor the shadow that falls from the gods,
can give the lie to his luminous praising.

He is one of the enduring messengers
carrying his bowl of praiseworthy fruit
well beyond the thresholds of the dead.

R.M. Rilke
Tr. J.M.E.

Orpheus' paean of praise may be considered a spiritual teaching, if not an explicit religious formula. We must understand that the aesthetic and religious have been so interwoven in human history that to try to pull them asunder seems like an irrational undertaking. And Orpheus did indeed play a significant role, which can be traced through later centuries, in the religious life of Greece. The course life offers is rough, as Orpheus knew only too well, his own having been full of grief. Prometheus had given humankind hope—staunch, resilient, energized hope—a mainstay of survival, to be sure. Orpheus offered humans a more comprehensive and actively creative response to the constant losses life brings and a more intimate and sense-oriented relationship with nature. As support for these life-guiding values, he offered specific prescriptions for humans to live by.

This teaching is most apparent in Orpheus' involvement in the mystery cult or cults which bear his name. Dionysus was the divinity most venerated in Thrace, and Orpheus was a follower of his religious teaching. However, Orpheus presented an alternative, an attempt to modify the excesses of the orgiastic and violent enthusiasm of the Bacchic rites. As it says in the Orphic *Argonautica*, "What the Bacchics may attain by orgies, Orpheus attains by his music which causes the grass to grow again."[3] Orpheus' legacy has survived in writings collectively referred to as *Orphica*: his theogony; the Orphic mysteries; and his poetic writings or Orphic hymns.[4]

Let us first consider his theogony. In the beginning, Orpheus taught, was Night, who brought forth the Cosmic Egg from which emerged Eros, "a dazzling light," also called Phanes or Erikepaios. Then Eros separated Heaven and the clouds from Earth and the ocean. Of these two parents, Heaven and Earth, the gods and humankind were generated. The Cosmic Egg is often referred to as the Orphic Egg; however, as a symbol for creation, it can be traced in mythology to many parts of the world— one might dare say "naturally." All of these original forces and elements were renamed in various versions of the story, which makes the telling less than clear. However, there is a universal sweep here which relates this creation progression to the theogonies of other peoples of the world.

To this creation story were added doctrines of the Orphic mysteries and prescriptions for his followers to live by, such as dietary rules. Animal flesh and blood were to be avoided—in fact, all killing was taboo. From this followed that neither fur nor wool should be worn. Since all precepts for a pure life, of course, made living more complicated and full of potential pitfalls, many forms of purification procedures were provided for the follower. For past offenses and errors, absolution was possible by means of priestly services and ceremonies. Following these precepts promised a better life in this world and the prospect of a good and happy life after death.

A clear definition of any of the many mystery cults in Greece and Southern Italy, all of which enjoined secrecy, is impossible. The designation "Orphic," a term of great antiquity, seems to have become a catchall type of phrase for any mysterious phenomenon which defied verbal exposition. What all the mystery cults had in common can be traced to the age-old veneration of the established mysteries at

Eleusis and the secrecy which shrouded them. Since one of the few facts we know about Eleusis is that Demeter guided its mystic procedures, we are led to believe they were derived from ancient mother goddess cults. Certainly the Furies had survived, and the Fates and Destiny were still hoveringly alive to Greek dramatists. Such ur-old figures are difficult to dispose of, even when, like Athena they are reintegrated and reborn in full armor. In any case, it is surprising to learn that ritual remnants of earlier cultures still existed in centers of clear-headed rationality like Athens, and may even have been respected, since many outstanding citizens had been initiated into these rites.

The Orphic mysteries, we are led to imagine, may have consisted of the singing or reciting of hymns extolling nature and the myths, and probably also included a religious drama, which perhaps also incorporated a sacrifice—though never an animal offering, of course. This ceremony was accompanied by prayer and purification. The mystery to be remembered and celebrated was that of the murder and dismemberment of the infant god Dionysus by the Titans, who then ate his flesh. The child was restored to life at the intervention of Apollo and Athena. The Titans were destroyed by Zeus, and from their remains, mankind was formed. Since the Titans had incorporated the god, humans inherited both Titan elements and a godlike component. This resulted in the mixture of good and evil in human beings and their need for expiation—purification in life so that in death their souls might find their way to a heavenly resting place.

Over the years, one element in this dramatic and

still very mysterious ceremony has baffled serious recorders from Plato to Clement of Alexandria. When they came bent on his murder, the Titans, so the story goes, managed to distract the young child Dionysus and keep him from crying out by offering him toys to play with. Ancient, mystic caskets have been found containing spinning tops of different sorts, knuckle bones, mirrors, balls, and dolls or "toys that bend their legs." Sacred cakes were included in the caskets, and bull roarers, proverbially used for their unearthly sound effects, were also found. Exactly how all these toys and other things were used is not clear. Plato simply says, a bit deprecatingly perhaps, that the mysteries were made up of sacrifice with prayer and some of "the pleasures of childish play." And the early Christian Fathers were horrified at such "silly" behavior in a sacred mystery.[5] But the mysteries endured; they supported the hope of reincarnation after death in an existence other than that of the wraithlike shades in the dark depths of Tartarus. Unlike the rationalist and the theologian, the artist in us all can find a deep satisfaction in the idea of adults reevoking playfulness and successfully becoming like little children while enmeshed in a celebration of life's deepest mysteries.

> The child's toys and the old man's reasons
> Are the final fruits of all the seasons.
>
> (to misquote Blake)

Among the collection of manuscripts known as *Orphica* are texts which have been discovered, principally in Italy, in ancient grave sites presumed to have been Orphic. Recent findings, which have been verified as authentically Orphic, include the *Derveni Papyrus*, and gold plate from Thessaly on which a poetic inscription is offered in two voices—that of the neophyte (recently arrived) and that of the receiving heavenly being:

> Parched with thirst am I, and dying.
>
>> Nay, drink of Me, the ever-flowing Spring
>> Where on the right is a fair cypress.
>
> Who art thou? Where art thou?
>
>> I am the son of Earth and of star-filled Heaven,
>> But from Heaven alone is my house.[6]

Generally, these gold plate inscriptions provided instruction and encouragement for souls on their journey after death.

To trace such a legacy as that of the Orphic teachings is to undertake to sort out the worn threads in an ancient tapestry. This effort has been and still is admirably pursued by scholars. Let us not tarry here for too long, however, examining the back side of the fabric with all its knots and telltale bits and pieces of colored threads, but rather keep our eyes on the bold if somewhat faded outlines of the intended presentation.

Sonnets to Orpheus
I
6

Does he really belong here? No, out of both
realms, the breadth of his nature grew.
More knowledgeably the willow's branches may be bent
by one who is intimate with the willow's roots.

On going to bed, leave on the table
no bread and no milk; they attract the dead.
But he, the conjuror, may well settle
under the softness of eyelids

there reflecting everything seen;
the magic of earth scent and rue
for him as true as the clearest bond.

Nothing can spoil for him the valid image;
be it from graves, be it from rooms,
though his praise fall on finger-ring, clasp, or jug.

R.M. Rilke
Tr. J.M.E.

Personages of such antiquity as Orpheus tend to increase in dimension and simultaneously blur their outlines as time passes. Let us give the widest possible scope to Orpheus' legacy by considering that his roots were shamanistic in origin. Such roots are ancient; indeed, we are speaking of a time before consciousness was separated into two branches: the rational brain versus the metaphysical, intuitive imagination. Shamanism combines diverse elements common to all religions close to nature and to human nature. One basic shamanistic assumption is that all living things, which we often destroy in order to live, have souls and must be treated with appropriate respect and even reverence.

Shamans lead us to the awareness that the heights above, the earth itself, and the depths below are all integral aspects of the world, a world that provides enlarged living space for human beings and a liberation from the mundane. The heights offer rapture and ecstasy, the depths a wholeness of experience—both realms are timeless, rich and expansive. These directions—high, level, and low—are very familiar to us. All those worthy things to which we aspire we set up in high places where the light is bright, even dazzling. Evil, cruelty, and fear are relegated to the depths below, where despair lurks. When we despair we head downward and then struggle to climb up again.

Eliade tells us, "In a general way, shamanism defends life, health, fertility, the world of 'light,' against death, diseases, sterility, disaster, and the world of 'darkness.'"[7] Shamans everywhere, and they have been worldwide, virtually fight battles against the powers of darkness, illness, anxiety, depression, and dread. Using all the potentials of sound and rhythm, they sing, dance, strum, and drum. With wind, water, earth, and fire they challenge the enemy. Offering ritual objects, beads, bowls, and bundles of teeth, fur, bones, and shells, they undertake to break the hold on human lives of the negative weight of guilt, sorrow, envy, and hatred.

With visits to the underworld and into the realm of nightly dreams, shamans undertake to open human consciousness into the veiled areas of existence which daily life and its demands close off, especially when a pressured need for achievement is the driving force. Opening these areas frees the imagination and creative energies for the expression of poetry, dance, song—all the arts—and for festival, carnival, theater, and ritual. Naturally, dance and trance have always been central features of shamanism and remain so today as universal approaches to the experience of ecstasy.

Adults need to play—play with, enjoy, and lose themselves in the small elemental things of earth. Children are closer to the worlds of the shaman than are most adults. They can cross boundaries between the realms more simply and easily. Theirs are the clouds above to float on, from which they may reach out to touch and toss the stars. And they can dare the dark stony depths, where monsters like overgrown bugs may be met and perhaps befriended. It's awesome and fun to be a little scared. Playfulness and absurdity distance young and old from the stuffy negativism of well-worn daily ways of being.

A sinking into the depths of despair in order to

find release from burdens of guilt, shame, and doubt may also at times be necessary. The intervention of powerful, sometimes witty animals with supernatural attributes may be evoked for help. They are capable of magically lightening the painful burden, enabling the heavy-laden sufferer to manage the climb back into earthy actuality.

When the reaction to unbearable pain is longed-for release, perhaps in flight, the healer may invoke and strengthen ties of mutuality and a sense of belonging through compassion and forgiveness. The entire family, at times even the whole clan of the sufferer, may be included in the ritualized healing process of drawing back the estranged, lost member. And what are the gains from such a healing journey? They may be too idiosyncratic to list, but there are possible gains for anyone: a better experiential sense of the strength down underneath that supports one's feet on the earth; perhaps also a greater appreciation of the warmth and support of others who, too, must accept the inevitability of loss minute by minute and, in so doing, learn to cherish and attend to the fullness and joy of each moment of time as it passes.

Our western culture has so rationalized, sweetened, and Calvinized our religious consciousness and practice that we now term much of all that is nature-bound or really human, "supernatural." Awe and wonder are suspect, and ecstasy is relegated to the province of the psychiatrist. Who then, in our midst today, represents and wears the costume of shaman? Who plays the role of mystic, the one who creates a matrix which combines both spheres of experience—who grows "out of both realms," as Rilke has phrased it? Should we not include the priest, the rabbi, the preacher, the teacher-mentor, and the healer as the shamanlike figure who stands as intercessor, as a bridge between divinity and humanity? When combined with artistic integrity, creativity itself has shamanistic power, a transcendent power actualized in the work of great artists through the centuries.

In our day, we take the recording of sound—vocal, instrumental, orchestral, and choral—so for granted that we fail to marvel at how enriched our lives are by this innovation. We can still hear the great Caruso sing, and recordings of Bach's glorious musical creations are readily available. But we can only guess, using our most imaginative ears, how it may have been to hear Orpheus as he enthralled all nature. His power with music was claimed to be mysterious and compelling—his words poetry and his voice itself spellbinding. Healing was present, quiet healing for mind and body. Beyond the account of Orpheus' descent into the underworld, this charm and healing power of his song gives credence to our claim of Orpheus' shamanistic roots.

How is it that words are so powerful, especially in the form of poetry? Language and touch are two forms of communication, two ways to bridge the space between us, that human beings have mastered. Whereas touch demands proximity, language and the voice can reach across space and touch the listening ear. Without language it is almost impossible to present an idea, to respond with an alternative, to discuss or arbitrate. Without dialogue, without communication, only physical force is really persuasive, and violence, as history demonstrates, breeds primarily hatred and more violence.

In the beginning we must, like other animals, have had grunts, cries, and maybe purrs with which we communicated with one another. Then, as we slowly became erect, our arms were freed and we could perfect gesture and dance, and with petroglyphs, pictographs, and hieroglyphs we could record, recall, and celebrate. With enlightenment—light and fire, Prometheus' gifts—we developed written and spoken language. Strange to reflect that what we now see on world maps as straight black demarcation lines—lines that actually cross mountains and rivers, lakes and deserts—also mark areas where different languages are spoken. Those who live near these borders adjust by using a regional patois or blend of language with which they can communicate. Travelers, however, can be in trouble—two steps over the black line and one must again resort to grunts and gestures or some kind of sketch. Is the question mark universal? Early explorers made use of beads, shells, and small things of great beauty as conciliatory offerings denoting friendliness, as a universal coinage to introduce themselves and make a speechless, peaceful entry.

Language, then, is the extraordinary tool which both binds and separates us from nature and from one another. We communicate ad infinitum by means of all the devices of modern invention. Never in the past has such a momentous quantity of translation between languages been undertaken. But we speak with one another clearly and readily only when both speaker and hearer are really at home with nuances of the same language. Misunderstanding does more damage than deafness. The final cry of the world could well be "But we didn't understand," and it won't refer to the song, the picture, the dance, the music. It may well be the result of a fumbling, inappropriate, misunderstood *word*.

Words, when we finally coined them, were easier to remember when they rhymed or were given a rhythmic order; before writing was invented this was of great importance. So perhaps our first real language was rhythmic—poetry and metaphor plus rhyme—a language that could be collected and then recollected in the mind in order to communicate. No wonder then that the bards, the singers, and the mothers singing to their children should have been those who provided continuity of communication from one generation to the next and between communities.

When such figures—shaman, seer, poet, singer, musician—are memorialized in myth, song, poetry, or writing, they tend to become iconlike, archetypal. All who follow after acclaim them. Such a figure is Orpheus. He enters on the scene and is first recorded by name in Greece soon after writing was invented and established. He was especially acknowledged as one who bonded humankind to the earth—to nature and what have come to be called the natural sciences. His art was inclusive, embracing the elements and all natural forms, myth and all artistic communication. His is the only universal language overriding all those black lines on the map of the world—the arts communicate in their varied ways and serve as our consistent means of sharing our humanity.

No wonder, then, that the name Orpheus can be traced in the writings of the great poets, including Shakespeare, Goethe, and Wordsworth, from Ovid on to twentieth-century Rilke, and in the scientific works of Bacon, Darwin, and Linnaeus, to mention only a few great names revered by all. Orpheus binds all the arts with nature and the natural sciences in what Elizabeth Sewell terms "a biology of thinking—postlogical and inclusive."[8]

Nature was there in Orpheus' fingertips, and all living things felt included—even rocks, the winds in the sails at sea, and fish. They responded, as did human beings, to his songs praising the toughness and courage of allying with truth, the challenge of loss, the hope in renewal, birth, and death itself. In his search for Eurydice, as he passed down into the underworld, Orpheus had seen wonders: the massive strength in the rocky heart of the earth; the struggling groping of the moisture-seeking roots of great trees; the yearning stretch of the cracked grain toward light and air. The snakes, worms, and grubs he knew too—and he was at one with all. Like one reborn, on his return he had experienced the wonder of greenness, the brilliance of blossom, of cloud against sun-swept sky.

When Orpheus stepped over that blurry black line dividing Thrace from Greece, he came with his lyre of nine strings in honor of the nine muses, one of them being Calliope, his mother. The role of the muses was to maintain the creativity of artists who had dedicated themselves to perfecting the skills necessary to their chosen art, and also to maintain the artists' enthusiasm and productivity. Artists lean on their muses in times of drought and honor them gratefully when their work goes well.

The Greek muses claim our interest because they are not limited to the arts we spell with a capital A. *Urania*, muse of astronomy, inspired observers of the heavens who plotted the stars and kept track of the ever-changing moon. *Clio* inspired those bards who told and finally recorded the wonderfully wise myths which provided the basic history of ancient Greece. *Polyhymnia*, as her name implies, fostered song and hymns of praise to the gods and, on occasion, to valiant mortal heroes. *Melpomene* encouraged the writers of drama, those tragedians whose profound works drew crowds to the pervasive theaters, and writers of comedy relied on *Thalia*. *Euterpe* was the muse of vocal and instrumental music, and *Erato*, muse of lyric verse, was no doubt Sappho's muse. *Terpsichore* was the muse of that oldest of the arts, the dance, which gives free expression to joy or sorrow with the ever-present instrument, the body. And *Calliope*, Orpheus' mother, "she of the beautiful voice," muse of epic poetry, probably intoned or chanted with lyre accompaniment. Artists such as sculptors, architects, and painters, justly famous in Greece, were apparently not endowed with muse encouragement. Perhaps the populace provided adequate, appropriate stimulus for their creativity. However, all that we see and know of what was once Greece certainly attests to the success of these artists, who perhaps had other private sources of inspiration.

Orpheus' aunts and mother must, obviously, have played an important role in his upbringing, for his language was poetry, his song irresistible, and his playing of the lyre enchanting. But did Orpheus have a special muse, other than his mother and his aunts? Who laid her hand on his shoulder and whispered in his ear *how* his song should be sung? The muses themselves, however attentive and supportive, could never have been successful without persuasion—that intuitive sense of how and when to ignite the spark that is the vital source of the creative and empathic moment. Only Peitho knows and can teach the skills essential for the right tone, the subtle nuance of sound that lingers in the ear and changes the attitude and receptivity of the listener. Each muse, with her knowledge of appropriate form and her skill, could be wonderfully useful, but only extraordinary persuasion can distract human beings from their overriding affairs, lead them into a new frame of mind, command their attention, and empower their creative capacities, which demand intense concentration and dedication.

It was recognized in Greece that without the right word, the apt phrase, the exactly appropriate tone of voice, language was not persuasive. The correct remark delivered abrasively could be offensive and counterproductive. There was skill to be learned, and a goddess to be evoked and propitiated. Many speakers in the assemblies and on the theater stage implored Peitho for help. For it is the need to communicate with truth and conviction that demands persuasion. Persuasion engenders the communication that is inherent in all the arts—the arts' language. Each offering reaches out with self-giving, with a touch that seeks communion, mutuality.

When one sings, plays, or makes some thing, trying to produce the most perfect note or object that he or she and the instrument or tool can achieve, that product is then authentic and has an integrity of its own. The story of the man who loved his violin is a good example. He played it daily and often. Finally, his wife inquired, "Shamus, you play so devotedly, but couldn't you try another tune or even another note? You always play the same one." "My dear wife," he said tolerantly, "I only want to play that one note perfectly. It is so beautiful in itself and I have yet to bring out its full loveliness. Other people are still looking for their note, but I have found mine."

Performing or exhibiting for others is undertaken to convey the note or object in its quasi perfection, to communicate a respect and joy, and to evoke an appreciation of this offering. If the perfect phrase, note, object does not reach out to touch and change the attentive listener or observer, freeing that intaking mind if only briefly from enmeshing daily details, then the persuasion, the communication, has failed. When integrity of purpose is not present in the artist's offering it may not move us. Sometimes the product, carried out as nearly as possible quite faultlessly, is nevertheless cold and unmoving. In dance, the performance becomes expert gymnastics, the song a perfectly rendered series of notes—clear, on pitch, and in time, but lifeless. One may well admire skill and competence but remain unpersuaded, untouched.

We need to better understand this phenomenon of art transference. An age-old philosophical-musical word from India, *rasa*—the component of music or art which "takes you out and beyond yourself"— may throw more light on this process. *Rasa* is, the learned ones say, "of the earth," since it can be apprehended by the senses, like the subtlest of tastes. It is also beyond earthly experience in that it pertains to the holy, evoking reverence and the transcendent. All the arts share a potential for moving the artist, but dance and music, it has been claimed, are the earliest and the most natural sources of *rasa*, since they speak the language of the body—the body and its instrument, the voice.

The composer of music and the choreographer of dance must be inspired by an intention to offer their conception or experience to others through performance. Performance is the necessary actualization of the artists' vision. The performer, the vehicle, must be attuned to this intention. Finally, the audience must have a genuine sensory and emotional appetite to even apprehend what is being shared, to take in the offering with concentrated attention, and thus to "relish a pleasure unrelated to everyday life." I would suggest that the intention shared by the choreographer, the composer, and the performer is a form of persuasion: the deep wish to reach out to others who make up the audience, to generate the savored taste, the inspiration of the idea, the experience. And indeed then the offering does persuade, for the arts as language speak loudly of our all-human relatedness, our having, as we do, the same bodies, senses, and life stages, the same joys and sorrows, the whole gamut of human experience.

Of course, if all the elements included in this process were to become the conscious intention of all the participants, their efforts to create, perform, and receive with integrity might be inhibited. But certainly there is a genuine and conscious eagerness to be clearly heard as well as, no doubt, a deeply felt receptivity on the part of the eagerly attentive audience.

Let me share an experience with you—not a myth of ancient Greece or an Indian concept, but an event recorded in the twentieth century. I saw *Meetings with Remarkable Men*, Peter Brook's film about Gurdjieff, who witnessed the event. Near the beginning of the film we are shown a truly extraordinary scene. In a remote valley of the Caucasus, a tribal festival is taking place. A large group of people have gathered, and they mill around until a procession of elders appears in marvelous costumes and with even more remarkable, lived-in faces.

The elders form a seated semi-circle and act as a panel of judges for a traditional contest. Contestants gather casually and sit on the ground facing the elders. Carrying unusual musical instruments, each contestant will play or sing in turn. The musician who produces the sound, the melody, the notes that cause the austere mountains to echo in response will win.

Each player is attuned to the mystery of the moment. Each note soars with yearning, a clear, lovely calling to the waiting earth; each offering is moving in its own right. A breathless listening pervades the atmosphere—a reaching out for that "something" further, beyond.

Finally, one performance, the playing of only a few phrases of strange unworldly notes, reverberates from the mountains, summoning the response of the whole valley. The sound is indeed awesome—a vibrant and pervading echo, like a resounding chord. As the tremor fades, an equilibrium of silence follows so complete that even breathing seems intrusive. No word is spoken. A judge gestures and a young boy moves into the circle carrying a white lamb, which he wordlessly offers the winning musician. Beginning with the musicians, the whole group disperses with dignity. An ancient rite has verified the expectation that the power of music can be manifested by the earth herself.

The most moving moments of this scene are those of the silence at its close. A genuine reverence could only thus be expressed and shared. One might wish that appreciation could always elicit such a response, that clattering applause and shouted enthusiasm would not shatter a needed interval of silent absorption.

How deep-rooted and universal the love of music is! Even the deaf and those whose hearing is impaired respond to rhythm. Animals too, we are beginning to learn, communicate with sounds which to us are inaudible. An organic, developmental explanation seems reasonable. The innate response, perhaps in all mammals, to rhythm and sound must initially be aroused by the consistent and close heartbeat of the mother, who carries the embryo from conception until birth. This pervasive pulse is soon joined by the increasingly strong beat of the heart of the fetus itself, a more rapid beat juxtaposed to that of the mother. The sounds of earth and the environment eventually and increasingly may begin to penetrate the barrier of amniotic fluid and flesh. Voices, song, and perhaps instruments become dimly audible. Someday there will be methods to verify all this. Is there some explanation here for the amazing early capacities of the Mozarts and the Bachs? But after all, we don't need to be able to understand everything—music belongs to the miraculous.

The strange circumstances of Orpheus' death remain to be described. It is depicted in two scenes. In the first, he sits playing his lyre and singing, listened to attentively by Thracian men, recognizable by their non-Greek clothing. In the second, he is being attacked by Thracian women armed with a variety of weapons which look like household tools. They are furious. Orpheus defends himself with his harp but is outnumbered. The legend goes on to tell us that he was killed by these maenads, his body torn limb from limb and thrown into the river Hebrus, which carried his parts off to the sea. His head finally washed ashore on the island of Lesbos. There a shrine was established, which became a site of prophetic worship and pilgrimage. As one might expect, Lesbos itself became famous for its great poets. Other cities and towns in Greece and Thrace also claimed to be the sites of his burial place. Heroes often had a number of graves in ancient Greece; their presence was claimed and honored and considered propitious.

But how has this savage and violent death been accounted for? Orpheus was never described as anything but a gentle, wandering musician, singing and playing his lyre. He urged moderation in the or-

giastic Dionysian rites and a closer affinity to the more sober and lyrical Apollo. In the wild, cathartic Bacchic celebrations, the women seemed to have become more ecstatically involved than the men. After many libations to Dionysus, groups of these frenzied bacchantae tore around the mountainous Thracian countryside until exhausted. They were said, in their frenzy, to tear apart the animal sacrifice with their own hands. These festival occasions tolerated extreme license. Perhaps Thracian women had more than the usual frustrations to work off or had the special encouragement of Dionysus for their behavior at his bucolic festivals. Since Orpheus preached moderation of such orgiastic behavior, it is possible that these women were angry with him. They felt excluded and actually were excluded in many areas of life and festival. Although there are many possible interpretations and symbolic readings, this is perhaps the most satisfying rationale that has been offered for the violent, murderous attack on Orpheus.

OPPOSITE, ABOVE.
Orpheus with Thracian men.

Thracian women attack and kill Orpheus.

His head, they claim, went on singing—perhaps still does if hearing is acute and ears receptive. His lyre was rescued by Apollo and placed in the heavens as a starry constellation—a luminous beacon.

Perhaps Orpheus' mysteries have endured because we feel a deep need to be in contact with the ever elusive experiences of life that are outside and beyond rational explanation; there is a yearning for a vaguely sensed, ephemeral state which eludes yet sometimes touches and surprises—lights and lifts. One can experience such a glimpse—individual, intimate, and seldom sharable—in a dream fragment or in a moment of arresting wonder.

Orpheus endures—an iconlike figure, a great benefactor of humankind; his name itself is evocative. It is a resonant name that has lived on in the voice, on the lips, and in the ear for close to three thousand years—from before there was a written alphabet until today. He was never forgotten by the Greeks, and the Romans adopted and celebrated him. Early Christianity incorporated his image, the Middle Ages dramatized and loved him, and artists of all ages have heard his message, have been inspired and done him honor.

Shamans have come and gone both named and unnamed, gods have emerged and disappeared over time; but something tantalizingly mystical and half understood about Orpheus captures the imagination and touches the deep human hunger for the aesthetic, for song, poetry, dance, and the hope engendered by prophecy—Orpheus the renowned and beloved poet, musician, and mystic. We can only marvel at the resounding echoes his name still evokes.

Sonnets to Orpheus
I
5

Erect no gravestone. Only let the rose
fully bloom each year in his memory.
For it is Orpheus—His metamorphosis
in this and that. We should not trouble

about other names. Once and for all
it's Orpheus, when it sings. He come and goes.
Isn't it already much, when at times he lingers over
the bowl of roses for a day or so?

O how vanishing he must be so that you understand!
Even though he himself takes fright that he may disappear.
In that his word transcends his being here,

already he is where you cannot follow.
Nor do the lyre strings force his hands.
For he obeys, even as he steps beyond.

R.M. RILKE
TR. J.M.E.

Orpheus

There is a great open space, a sunset sky, an open, curved horizon broken only by three huge hayricks. A vague footpath leads through the spread of fields—nothing else breaks the uncluttered space suffused with golden light.

Two figures stand close together sharing a thought, a secret: Orpheus in a long, dark garment holding and playing his lyre, and beside him, his muse—a white-clad, angel-like figure, wings half folded behind long, flowing red-gold hair.

They are very intimate. Peitho whispers, "Sing, Orpheus, of the fading daylight that was beautiful and is lost. Sing the world to quiet, healing sleep that it may be ready to meet the coming day with purposeful hope and song."

Orpheus and his muse.

Sonnets to Orpheus
I
19

Yet fast as the world changes
like massing cloud forms,
all perfected things fall
homeward to the primeval.

Above the change and the way,
wider and freer,
your prelude song endures,
god with the lyre.

Sufferings are not understood,
loving is not yet learned,
and that which estranges in death

is not unveiled.
Alone the song over the land
hallows and praises.

R.M. RILKE
TR. J.M.E.

Socrates

Perhaps no name evokes more respect, even intellectual awe, than that of Socrates. Born in Athens in 469 B.C., he lived an idiosyncratic life until 399 B.C. when, at the age of seventy, he was prosecuted and condemned to death by the Athenians. Through the ages he has been extolled as the wisest man, the philosopher-teacher of ancient Greece who sacrificed himself for Truth. He is still venerated as a martyr and a man of great insight and integrity.

Is this how the Athenians regarded him during his lifetime? Actually, we might never have heard of him, or perhaps heard only obliquely through the writings of his students, if he had not been condemned to death. A dramatic death is often the final, memorable event in the account of a legendary figure. Athens paid little attention to Socrates through most of his lifetime. Considered an eccentric character and a great talker, he was disregarded by his city. To his fellow citizens he seemed to play the role of town joker, a kind of philosopher-sophist who gathered around himself the idle, rich young blades of the town and led them into discussion of rather vague ideas. He was the butt of the comic dramatists, the fool. Aristophanes, who was his friend, focused his comic play *The Clouds* on him and involved him as a character in three other productions. Socrates surely laughed with the crowd. He prided himself on being a gadfly and he played a prominent role in city gossip.

Though he was often to be found near the public buildings and seemed eager for an audience, he was in fact a very private person. Moderate in all his pleasures, poor and of low-to-middle-class status, he was nevertheless quite independent and proud. His father was a stonecutter—an artist or artisan—and his mother a midwife, both honorable but humble professions. He and they were law-abiding Athenian citizens.

Socrates acknowledged the gods of the city and took part in religious observances and festivals, but considered himself, beyond that, to be specially guided by his own *daimones*. These soothsaying divine beings served as personal spirit messengers who prohibited him from inappropriate or unworthy actions or words. This, he seemed to claim, made him a protégé of higher beings; there is little doubt that he felt special and no doubt at all that he felt superior. Being a philosopher licensed one to free speech, he maintained; however, he did not advocate it for the masses, even though Athens prided herself on such freedom for all citizens.

No very clear description of Socrates exists, but the few remarks recorded about his appearance indicate that he was outstandingly ugly. A statue of Socrates has survived which depicts him as a rather short, sturdy man, barefoot as he always was,

Socrates.

wrapped in the loose toga of a city dweller. His face is round, surrounded by a crop of hair and beard, his nose rather flat and unaristocratic. His stolid, unremarkable figure must, however, have become dramatically alive when he began to speak. In one of the few surviving verbal descriptions of Socrates' appearance, one of his followers, Alcibiades, is quoted as saying, laughingly and with affectionate admiration, "[Socrates] bears a strong resemblance to those figures of Silenus in the statuaries' shops . . . they are hollow inside, and when they are taken apart you see that they contain little figures of gods."[1] Apparently the Silenus figures are very ugly but the gods within them are of gleaming gold. We are offered, then, the figure of a man who falls far short of the average standard for good stature—stature as judged relative to the norm of a community. However, his innermost qualities, when revealed, display a brilliant treasure of pure gold. This purest of metals is malleable, never dulls or tarnishes, endures forever, and is as rare as true beauty.

The artists of Greece found such pleasure in the symmetry and grace of the human body, producing the many sculptures, figures, and paintings of great beauty known to us, that we may be persuaded the Greeks were a remarkably handsome people. Their support of early physical training in the gymnasium and keen interest in Olympic champions testifies to their aesthetic appreciation of well-built bodies. How was the dominant stress on physical perfection actually pursued in Greece? Were deformities eliminated at birth? Was it the grave duty of midwives to make decisions concerning appropriateness and perfect fitness? Infanticide was an accepted practice, and in times of famine, the problem of too many girl babies was forthrightly solved. Fathers had absolute power over their children, including life and death. Proud families maintained high standards for their offspring. Status and honors were showered on Olympic champions and gave support to the gymnastic training offered to all young men. Sculptors sought out perfectly developed bodies to pose as models. The output of this artwork must have been prodigious if we consider how much has indubitably been destroyed. The remaining objects of art are among our greatest treasures and our paragons of physical beauty.

Along with their passion for the beauty of the human form, there is strong evidence in their art that the Greeks were fascinated by the grotesque; both large and small statues of deformed bodies have been retrieved from Greek ruins. The abnormal may, according to the law of opposites, offset the perfect; the unlovely may highlight the beautiful. Human beings seem to find ugliness attractively abhorrent. We flock to see physical aberration at the sideshow —the dwarf, the fat lady, the Siamese twins, the two-headed calf. We love clown figures with their snub noses, great mouths, and mournful eyes, and enjoy their antics at the circus, when not at too close quarters.

The Greeks, in their playfully creative wisdom, incorporated the grotesque and abnormal into their pantheon and the myths which were their history and delight. Animal and human forms were combined in their nature divinities, and the Centaurs, the Cyclopes, and Pan were lively, bizarre creatures. Medea was portrayed as upsettingly awful, and they

say that the Furies, in their vindictive rage, fright-
ened the audience into a panic when *Orestes* was
played in the theater. What an enviable, even child-
like wisdom this parade of fantastic creatures presents! When monsters are grotesque, a creative shift
can recast them into playful entities. The frightening
grizzly bear becomes your best friend, Teddy. The
world over, through myth, fairy tale, and the arts,
the wise old ones and imaginative children have per-

Head of a satyr.

formed this alchemy for us. We do well to preserve and cherish this potential and prize it in the rich legacy of Greece.

But to find oneself endowed with a grotesque feature is a different matter. We all have suffered in empathy for Pinocchio, Struwwelpeter, and, of course, Cyrano de Bergerac. Children are all too regularly put down when their appearance is compared by adults to that of siblings or others in their peer group. Nothing could be more undermining and belittling, since physical flaws are seldom reparable. If, as a child, Socrates suffered from the shame of ugliness, it probably later became a goad for his intellectual and spiritual development.

We need not look far for evidence of how prevalent shame concerning physiognomy is in this world. The phrase "to save face" is understood everywhere and justifies extreme measures of self-defense and retaliation. As a small boy Socrates may have hidden his face and avoided uncomfortable encounters. Later, taking courage from his developed physical capacities, he may have become more bold; encouraged, one would hope, by his capable father, he would learn to hold his ground against peer aggressors. Our clues and guesses come only from observing the young in present-day playgrounds and street corners and from the childhood memories told to psychologists and school counselors. The truly transcendent resolution of a lifelong stigma, such as that of Cyrano's nose, is to develop a skill to such a degree that it becomes an original virtuosity. This, I would suggest, was Socrates' creative resolution.

Socrates' most lethal weapon became his subtle

wit and the refutation of others in negative dialogue. At times, the complacent stupidity of others goaded him to exasperation. An overconfident young man would be lured by Socrates into argument. Professing a humble wish to learn, Socrates would then slowly pull the rug out from under every foothold on which the unwary opponent rested his argument. Frustration and exposure to ridicule resulted for the victim. These were probably exhilarating victories for a man who had, perhaps from childhood on, felt himself exposed to ridicule and shame in a world of beautiful potential heroes. We admire Socrates' repeated exhibition of verbal dexterity. Such fencing, however, tends to silence rather than promote free and open discussion. Socrates froze opinionated adversaries into stubborn opposition in their effort to save their wounded self-respect. He made enemies of the hoi polloi, and even the five hundred jurors at his trial were whipped with his sharp sarcasm. Such an approach to discussion and problem-solving is, of course, not the way of true persuasion—the way of Peitho in her most upright form. Neither is false humility used as a trap. Socrates was not humble. On such occasions he was not honestly trying to persuade an opponent to take another view, to consider, if only temporarily, its virtues and defects; he showed no intention of discussing with an open mind. If we enjoy the performance, it isn't to our credit. This teasing, trickster role did, however, become a prevailing image of Socrates in his time and for many years to come.

Plato, one of the reporters responsible for this image, also offers us another, more positive aspect of this complicated man—that of Socrates as a great and loving teacher. Socrates devoted himself to seeking out promising young men to become his students. His followers often seem to have been won in intimate settings. They were young men searching for intellectual stimulus, some way of life other than the well-worn route to physical heroism. Socrates took pleasure in their physical beauty, but he also persistently stressed nobility of spirit and dedication to truth as the highest good. He was a devoted friend and master to the young men of Athens and also revealed poetic qualities which offset his "quilled porcupine" response to self-assured stupidity. Here one may remember his poetic invocation to Pan and his prayer to become beautiful in the inner man.

The accumulation of knowledge itself was not Socrates' focus. His aim was to stimulate, to liberate the processes of thinking in the still-flexible minds of his young followers. Socrates encouraged the young men to exercise their minds, as the gymnasium stretched and exercised their bodies, in order to achieve the mobility of a living relationship with being and truth. Such exercise proceeds and progresses in the mind by evoking inner tension which must consistently be resolved in order to arrive at an equilibrium. The apt teacher or mentor joins the student in this effort to find resolution and strength. By promoting a process of exploration, horizons and potentials of which the student had not been aware may be stretched to reveal a way of being. This constant exercise of faculties, also fostered by myths and legends and a lively curiosity, leads to the discovery of an order of existence and the values which give meaning to human lives. Every true mentor recognizes and validates this process. Change and growth are the goals of teaching; knowledge is its by-product.

Philosophy offers such a vigorous training, and those who undertake it must be devoted and keen to pursue the course. It is touching to learn that Socrates' students spoke of being "in philosophy," immersed in a process as a way of being. For the young, and the old as well, there is something wonderful about becoming involved, about knowing that you are in the presence of greatness—that you are part of the striving in the human story. It can be a serious statement nowadays when a young student says "I am into" literature or psychology or whatever, a statement not to be taken lightly.

Plato, himself being one of the consistently attentive members of Socrates' group of young scholars, speaks of him with intimacy and genuine appreciation. Great poet, philosopher, and teacher that he was, Plato has left us masterpieces of biography in the *Symposium*; a memorial document of Socrates' death in the *Phaedo*; and a celebration of Socrates' life by way of his own prolific career. It is largely through this loyal and gifted student that Socrates has survived as a venerated mentor. If Plato refrained from any direct criticism of his master, it obviously must have been because his greatness was more impressive than his faults and failures.

As a late-adolescent, Plato came under the aegis of this man whose ideas would dominate his creative work as a philosopher throughout his long life. Like other young men of affluence and good family, Plato might have prepared himself more readily according to the heroic mode, then so admired and supported by Greek ambitions. In late adolescence, this emerging young adult reached out to a model, a living person who seemed to firmly embody the characteristics he held most high. The evidence that such persons exist or have existed gives stamina to the young and supports their determination to emulate, to follow in well-worn footsteps. That such a tendency can be misdirected into gang membership and fascist organization is a well-documented hazard. In any case, the need to focus youthful, zestful fidelity on a person or cause can, at this point in development, be invested with genuine fervor.

The pressure of society is toward the norm. We applaud the well-adjusted young who go through all the developmental stages with flying colors, who rationally accept the bounties available and the limits demanded. These will, we argue, become good, stable citizens who will pass the existing values on to their children. Rebels are frowned on, raise problems, and demand special attention—just as Socrates' young followers, and Plato among them, found themselves under scrutiny by the more conservative elements in Athens. Yet without such determined misfits, an impetus for growth and positive, creative change would be lost; not even the smug, status-quo-ish optimist thinks society is perfect.

Plato was from an old, aristocratic family of able men, both noble and ignoble, but powerful. Wealthy and intelligent, his initial goal was to become a tragic dramatist, and surely drama is one of the most effective sources of the leaven which society consistently needs for its health in a world of constant change. He eventually turned his whole attention to philosophy, but only after the death of Socrates. Fully persuaded by Socrates' precepts and teaching, Plato dedicated himself to writing so that new and great ideas could be passed on to those who had the leisure and could afford to come to his academy for philosophers. By means of study, honest debate, and exposure to the thinking of the great minds of the past, students could open themselves to persuasion. Plato made the teachings of his mentor the foundation for his own work and a legacy for thinkers of the future.

Whether Plato's presentation of his adored teacher was entirely unbiased or not, his literary and dramatic genius produced a tragic hero of such greatness that we can only be silenced by the nobility of his persuasive logic and grateful for his life. We need such venerable models as Socrates. The depths to which human beings can sink are frightening, a fact which the twentieth century has compellingly demonstrated. We are in desperate need of the highest stars to show us our positive capacities and offer us hope and courage. Let us now turn to some of Plato's writings to sort out what truly concerned Socrates. We must try to master the dance as well as revere the dancer.

First, it may be salutary to view Socrates' logical method in relation to that of other thinkers dealing with the interpretation of subjective evidence. The topics Socrates undertakes to set on firm foundations are vast, amorphous, yet of vital importance to him and his way of life, the way of the philosopher: what is truth, the beautiful, the idea, essence, justice. That Socrates dealt so often with such matters is understandable, since he was really only interested in human beings and how they function—in their lives, ideals, and relationships, in their sense of community living. Scientific exploration and data he found boring and of little use; these promoted none of the virtues necessary for a good life, for the development of noble human beings living in community.

But how does one go about describing and interpreting something which has no sensory factuality? From a clinical perspective, the phrase that has been coined to address this issue is *disciplined subjectivity*. It describes a method by which subjective evidence may be selected, sorted out, and gathered into a persuasive whole—into an acceptable and sturdy, if not factually proven, assessment. If a number of clues seem to support a hypothesis, it may be at least tentatively convincing; although never fully arriving at certainty, the hypothesis may be *approaching* the truth. For example, if a group of eminent scholars find humor to be a particularly striking trait of all the wisest individuals they have studied, they may, within reason, decide that humor is an attribute of wisdom. Disciplined subjectivity is mandatory for the inward process of the thinker himself. Clear, disciplined thinking, a dialogue in the mind of the thinker, is necessary in order to discover and exclude prejudgment and to honestly seek the goal of the quest. Although never completely free of bias, one must cultivate an awareness of one's own biases in order to inflict them less destructively and haphazardly in the search for truth.

Socrates, our model philosopher, often surveys a wide field, a broad base of interrelated phenomena to justify his formulations. At other times, he vigorously questions and pares down the subject under consideration in order to establish a solid footing on which to construct reasonably grounded fact. It is possible to follow Socrates through these processes in the discourses of Plato's *Symposium*, which we will now consider.

Plato describes a dramatic event in which a number of well-known Athenian luminaries take part. This symposium takes place at the home of Agathon, a tragic poet who has just won a prize in a drama competition. All those present are friends and admirers of Socrates, and he sits beside his host, a place of honor. It is a celebration, and a warm, friendly spirit prevails. They decide to spend the evening eating and drinking as usual, but then, as entertainment, they will also have a discourse on the chosen topic of Love (Eros), each person speaking in turn. Socrates speaks last, and, just as he concludes, Alcibiades bursts in with drunken companions and makes a final speech in honor of Socrates. The gathering disperses, but Socrates does not leave until early dawn, still fresh and sober. Plato records all this, in a lively style, as a rather normal evening of entertainment in Athens in 416 B.C.

The presentation by Socrates provides a detailed example of his exacting, didactic method. Here he is concerned more with drawing out and promoting a process of change and real learning in the pupil than with just winning the argument. Learning by rote, heaping up information, and acquiring answers without thinking them through do nothing to change one's convictions, to develop the "inner man."

In the *Symposium*, Socrates' remarks immediately follow those of Agathon. As he begins, he does not challenge Agathon, but gently leads him to see the error of his assumptions. Agathon is not opinionated; he responds quietly, accepting Socrates' corrections. Agathon's motive had been to say something beautiful, poetic, even creative, but he was in no way pretentiously arrogant. Socrates begins questioning Agathon in a slow, precise manner which brings about complete surrender.

SOCRATES
Is the nature of Love (Eros) such that he must be love *of* something, or can he exist absolutely without an object?

(Agathon agrees that an object is necessary.)

SOCRATES
And does [Love] desire and love the thing that he desires and loves when he is in possession of it or when he is not?

AGATHON
Probably when he is not.

SOCRATES
If you reflect for a moment, you will see that it isn't merely probable but absolutely certain that one desires what one lacks, or rather that one does not desire what one does not lack . . . Because a man who possesses a quality cannot be in need of it . . . Now recall also what it was that you declared in your speech to be the object of Love. I'll do it for you, if you like. You said, I think, that the troubles among the gods were composed by love of beauty, for there could not be such a thing as love of ugliness. Wasn't that it?

AGATHON
Yes.

SOCRATES
Quite right, my dear friend, and if that is so, Love will be love of beauty, will he not, and not love of ugliness?

(*Agathon agrees*)

SOCRATES
Now we have agreed that Love is in love with what he lacks and does not possess.

AGATHON
Yes.

SOCRATES
So after all Love lacks and does not possess beauty?

AGATHON
Inevitably.

SOCRATES
Well then, would you call what lacks and in no way possesses beauty beautiful?

AGATHON
Certainly not.

SOCRATES
Do you still think then that Love is beautiful, if this is so?

AGATHON
It looks, Socrates, as if I didn't know what I was talking about when I said that.

SOCRATES
Still, it was a beautiful speech, Agathon. But there is just one more small point. Do you think that what is good is the same as what is beautiful?

AGATHON
I do.

SOCRATES

Then, if Love lacks beauty, and what is good coincides with what is beautiful, he also lacks goodness.

AGATHON

I can't find any way of withstanding you, Socrates. Let it be as you say.

SOCRATES

Not at all, my dear Agathon. It is *truth* that you find it impossible to withstand; there is never the slightest difficulty in withstanding Socrates.[2]

Socrates, now finished with his close and persistent questioning of Agathon, moves right into an account of Love "which [he] once heard from a woman of Mantinea, called Diotima." He adds, "The easiest thing will be to go through the same questions and answers as she did with me . . . she employed against me the arguments by which I demonstrated to Agathon that to my way of thinking Love is neither beautiful nor good."[3] There is no way to really prove that Diotima is an invention of Socrates, but she does proceed to debate and argue in the precise fashion that has always been ascribable to Socrates and it is very easy to convince oneself that he is speaking to himself. In fact, he even suggests that he and she "employ" the same manner of argumentation.

The symposium continues with this exchange between Diotima and Socrates, which offers revealing insight into Socrates' development. Selected passages relevant to our understanding of Socrates' probable "hang-ups" are offered here in approximate sequence. The passages are quoted in detail so that

Socrates' meticulous method of "wearing down," as he develops the formulation of an idea, may again be illustrated.

SOCRATES
What do you mean, Diotima? Is Love ugly and bad?

DIOTIMA
Don't say such things, do you think that anything that is not beautiful is necessarily ugly?

SOCRATES
Of course I do.

DIOTIMA
And that anything that is not wisdom is ignorance? Don't you know that there is a state of mind halfway between wisdom and ignorance?

SOCRATES
What do you mean?

DIOTIMA
Having true convictions without being able to give reasons for them. Surely you see that such a state of mind cannot be called understanding, because nothing irrational deserves the name; but it would be equally wrong to call it ignorance; how can one call a state of mind ignorance which hits upon the truth? The fact is that having true convictions is what I called it just now, a condition halfway between knowledge and ignorance.

SOCRATES
I grant you that.

DIOTIMA
Then do not maintain that what is not beautiful is ugly, and what is not good is bad. Do not suppose that because, on your own admission, Love is not good or beautiful,

he must on that account be ugly and bad, but rather that he is something between the two.

SOCRATES
And yet, everybody admits that he is a great god.

DIOTIMA
When you say everybody, do you mean those who don't know him, or do you include those who do?

SOCRATES
I mean absolutely everybody.

(*Diotima bursts out laughing*)

DIOTIMA
Well, Socrates, I don't see how he can be admitted to be a great god by those who say that he isn't even a god at all.

SOCRATES
Who are they?

DIOTIMA
You are one of them and I'm another.

SOCRATES
What can you mean?

DIOTIMA
It's perfectly easy; you'd say, wouldn't you, that all gods are happy and beautiful? You wouldn't dare to suggest that any of the gods is not?

SOCRATES
Good heavens, no.

DIOTIMA
And by happy you mean in secure enjoyment of what is good and beautiful?

SOCRATES
Certainly.

DIOTIMA
But you have agreed that it is because he lacks what is good and beautiful that Love desires these very things.

SOCRATES
Yes, I have.

DIOTIMA
But a being who has no share of the good and beautiful cannot be a god?

SOCRATES
Obviously not.

DIOTIMA
Very well then, you see that you are one of the people who believe that Love is not a god.

SOCRATES
What can Love be then? A mortal?

DIOTIMA
Far from it.

SOCRATES
Well, what?

DIOTIMA
As in my previous example, he is halfway between mortal and immortal.

SOCRATES
What sort of being is he then, Diotima?

DIOTIMA
He is a great spirit, Socrates; everything that is of the nature of a spirit is half god and half man.

SOCRATES
And what is the function of such a being?

DIOTIMA
To interpret and convey messages to the gods from men and to men from the gods, prayers and sacrifices from the one, and commands and rewards from the other. . . . Spirits are many in number and of many kinds, and one of them is Love.[4]

Is it justifiable to think that Socrates longed to identify himself as such a spirit, halfway between mortal and immortal—such a messenger and teacher? His disdain for the sophists, who earned their living by teaching young men how to use language skillfully, often in order to avoid disclosing great ignorance, was well known. He might, therefore, have been happier to cast himself in the role of great spirit, as Diotima describes, than to be classed along with the slick sophist trainers of rhetoric.

We should pause to ask ourselves a number of questions. Why does Socrates introduce the figure of Diotima, a woman, into his argument? Is this introduction of a woman acting as his teacher meant to be humorous? It is hard to think otherwise, considering the male setting, and, as the argument proceeds, Socrates' humble "student" response must have added to the fun. Or was his method of discourse so ingrained that he needed another voice to carry it through, someone to fill the role of teacher so that he could, for once, take over the role of the student he claimed he always really was?

Or is it Socrates' deeply felt need of a wise woman's firm voice to state once and for all that ugly is not bad and that what is not beautiful is not necessarily ugly? Had some lack in his relationship with his mother played a role in his yearning for justification? Possibly, being herself in the business, she somehow felt that having an ugly baby was failure on her part. Babies, I believe, get all those messages—poor mother and poor Socrates. Feelings matter, and sometimes they interfere with that initial bonding mutuality that gives security and develops trust. As a grown man, Socrates perhaps still longed for a woman's voice to say clearly, "Snub noses are considered ugly, but they don't mean that you are not good. Good itself is beautiful. We think you're fine just as you are." In any case, shame may have been such a wounding element all through his youthful development that the scars remained painful and in need of healing.

Having made note at the beginning of this chapter of the importance of Socrates' ugliness in his life development, I find it happily justifying that these outspoken words from Socrates' own mouth—via Plato, of course—are so blatantly a topic of Socrates' own choosing. Socrates' invention of Diotima and the long discourse he presents to his friends should make us feel supported in believing that a stigma of ugliness did play a major role in his development. Good and bad, ugly and beautiful, had been intricately intermeshed and still demanded untangling. In order to make this issue an appropriate topic of a philosophic discussion, he needed to step back and make it Diotima's concern and not too obviously his own.

Diotima does one thing to win our hearts. In the midst of all this heavy talk, she bursts out laughing and follows this with an unexpected joke at Socrates' own expense—an amusing twist lightly leads the verbal fencing into a surprise touché for Diotima. She traps Socrates in a logical impasse such as those he himself loved to set. We may be particularly pleased by her laughter since Socrates' didactic mode often cries out for humor.

Further on in the *Symposium*, Socrates professes his great need for Diotima's teaching. In response, Diotima launches into a remarkable and concentrated exposition of development in the human life cycle. This passage reveals Socrates' perceptive awareness of his own development and the personal problems he was consciously facing at this stage of his life. In these passages, we are using twentieth-century hearing aids and listening to a no-longer-young Socrates taking stock of himself and looking forward into the future. We do well to remember also that his three sons were very young at the time of his death at seventy years of age, one an infant. He is at this point fifty-eight years old and clearly concerned with his own procreativity and immortality.

DIOTIMA

Now that we have established what love invariably is, we must ask in what way and by what type of action men must show their intense desire if it is to deserve the name of love. What will this function be? Can you tell me?

SOCRATES

If I could, Diotima, I should not be feeling such admiration for your wisdom, or putting myself to school with you to learn precisely this.

DIOTIMA
Well . . . I will tell you. The function is that of procreation
in what is beautiful, and such procreation can be either
physical or spiritual. . . . There is something divine about
the whole matter; in procreation and bringing to birth
the mortal creature is endowed with a touch of immortality. . . . The object of love, Socrates, is not, as you
think, beauty.

SOCRATES
What is it then?

DIOTIMA
Its object is to procreate and bring forth in beauty.

SOCRATES
Really?

DIOTIMA
It is so, I assure you. Now, why is procreation the object
of love? Because procreation is the nearest thing to perpetuity and immortality that a mortal being can attain.
. . . The same argument holds good in the animal world
as in the human, and mortal nature seeks, as far as may
be, to perpetuate itself and become immortal. . . . Even
during the period for which any living being is said to
live and to retain his identity—as a man, for example, is
called the same man from boyhood to old age—he does
not in fact retain the same attributes, although he is called
the same person; he is always becoming a new being
and undergoing a process of loss and reparation, which
affects his hair, his flesh, his bones, his blood, and his
whole body. And not only his body, but his soul as well.
No man's character, habits, opinions, desires, pleasures,
pains, and fears remain always the same; new ones come
into existence and old ones disappear. . . . It is in this
way that everything mortal is preserved; not by remaining forever the same, which is the prerogative of divinity,

but by undergoing a process in which the losses caused by age are repaired by new acquisitions of a similar kind. This device, Socrates, enables the mortal to partake of immortality, physically as well as in other ways; but the immortal enjoys immortality after another manner. So do not feel surprise that every creature naturally cherishes its own progeny; it is in order to secure immortality that each individual is haunted by this eager desire and love.

SOCRATES
You may be very wise, Diotima, but am I really to believe this?

DIOTIMA
Certainly you are . . . if you will only reflect you will see that the ambition of men provides an example of the same truth. You will be astonished at its irrationality unless you bear in mind what I have said, and remember that the love of fame and the desire to win a glory that shall never die have the strongest effects upon people. For this even more than for their children they are ready to run risks, spend their substance, endure every kind of hardships and even sacrifice their lives.[5]

Is this concluding statement by Diotima somehow prophetic—pointing to the final decisions of Socrates' life? We should remember that during this whole long presentation Socrates is speaking to himself as well as to his friends. It is an exposition of his own deepest concerns, and it becomes then, one might hazard, a dramatization of Socrates by Socrates, as recorded by Plato.

Socrates' understanding of the life cycle as a constant, ongoing process is, for the perpetrators of the "psychosocial human life cycle theory," very humbling as well as startling. He understood and described what is so difficult to teach, namely that there may be "crises" and "phases" and so called "steps," but the strength of the *process* is what may lead to wisdom in due time. Heraclitus, whose writings Socrates undoubtedly knew, was also clearly aware, even before Socrates, of "the simultaneous operation of contrary tensions" necessarily coexistent and essential for existence, strength and growth. When we accept these philosophers' intuitive grasp of concepts so vital to the life cycle theory—we do homage to the truth that there is nothing new under the sun.

If we follow Diotima's description of the process through which a man's life takes him and apply it to Socrates' own life, we gain a perspective on the development of this unusual man. If his voice and Diotima's are one and the same, as we have assumed, then he has observed in himself what most people fail to see—namely, that growth is a process offering constant challenges. Each growth stage, and every day, brings loss but offers new insight and opportunity. Vital strengths accrue, and some wisdom is the fruit of this learning, growing, losing process; along with this process emerges an acceptance of the finite nature and slow disintegration of physical being. For a fifty-eight-year-old man, successful and healthy, this is genuine maturity; it is even precocious, but perhaps not for sages. What could one point to in his early upbringing that might have nourished such a fortuitous development?

Midwifery, his mother's profession, demands skills and a willingness to take over an often precarious service at any time of day or night. Socrates refuted the title "teacher." He preferred to describe his work—enlightenment through discourse, the slow releasing and awakening of wisdom in his young followers—as the art of "midwifery." He referred also to the "travail," the pangs of birth, through which one must suffer to make progress in the search for truth. Socrates had obviously learned to honor such a dedicated, life-giving, and caring profession and emulated it in his own work.

Considering all the building that was proceeding in Athens, his father, the stonecutter, was probably a busy hardworking man. He was thrifty and capable, no doubt, for he left behind a legacy for his son and was able to send him to the gymnasium like the best and noblest youths of the city. Lucky Socrates! But, as we have pointed out, young Socrates had that one blatant misfortune of being conspicuously ugly in a beauty-worshiping milieu.

> Every adult, whether he is a follower or a leader, a member of a mass or an elite, was once a child. He was once small. A sense of smallness forms a substratum of his mind, ineradicably. His triumphs will be measured against his smallness, his defeats will substantiate it.[6]

When we think back we resonate with this truth and know how deeply we still experience our inadequacies and the shame that accompanies varieties of smallness.

As a young man, Socrates' rigorous training at the gymnasium plus his stubborn purposefulness resulted in noteworthy physical prowess, which comrades in battle like Alcibiades loved to relate. It was also claimed that Socrates could, on occasion, drink the night through and never show signs of weariness or drunkenness. Alcibiades offers a description of Socrates' phenomenal feats of physical endurance as a soldier in the army when they served together in the campaign against Potidaea:

> A problem occurred to [Socrates] early one day, and he stood still on the spot to consider it. When he couldn't solve it he didn't give up, but stood there ruminating. By the time it was midday people noticed him, and remarked to one another with wonder that Socrates had been standing wrapped in thought since early morning. Finally in the evening after dinner, some Ionians brought their bedding outside—it was summertime—where they could take their rest in the cool and at the same time keep an eye on Socrates to see if he would stand there all night as well. He remained standing until it was dawn and the sun rose. Then he made a prayer to the sun and went away.

Alcibiades concludes this story with this simple statement:

> . . . the really wonderful thing about him is that he is like no other human being, living or dead.[7]

It is tempting to imagine Socrates suddenly stopped in his tracks—it is reported that he often was—in order to have such a discourse with Diotima.

This story of Socrates depicts not only his capacity for physical endurance but also his incredible tenacity and mental concentration. In his maturity, Socrates made of philosophy a lifelong quest and inaugurated it as a mind science—a field of inquiry demanding an exacting commitment and devoted concentration to the exclusion of all other interests. We remember Socrates as inventor of the Socratic method—sharp Socratic surgery, the process through which the loving search for wisdom is carried on. Keep an open mind, be scrupulous in the search for truth, Socrates taught his followers; be rigorously disciplined yourselves and with all who would wish to learn from you. Everyone has moments of philosophizing. We ask ourselves what life is all about and why. But philosophers, the dedicated ones, are not at all casual about their quest. They get buried in the maze, the puzzle. They get "bitten" or "stung," as Socrates warns his pupils, and cannot let go. The Lady Wisdom, the Sophia they pursue, has had many names: Hochma, Devi Mahatma, Paraparamita, Pallas Athena. She is elusive and demanding, but her pursuers are ardent and court her persistently.

As a somewhat older man, dedicated to teaching, Socrates created a compatible prototype teacher, Diotima, with whom he carried on perhaps many dialogues on the subjects of beauty and the good, perpetuity and productivity—reproduction and spiritual creativity. These dialogues, one might imagine, involved a consistent sifting and sorting of possible grains of truth to be winnowed out from an assortment of useless hulls. Reflecting on development, Socrates maintained, as we have learned through Diotima, that life is a constant process of learning and change, an ongoing loving procreativity, both physical and spiritual, a bringing to birth in which "the mortal creature is endowed with a touch of immortality."

Socrates' persistent referral to procreativity, birth and rebirth, makes us again aware of his relationship to his own mother, the midwife. Whatever else may have been the subjects of lively conversation in his childhood milieu, certainly birth and details of bringing to birth must have been among the most constant and lively topics. But who played the role of midwife for Socrates and for the procreativity of his wisdom? In a creative person, the muses are attentively there—whispering, nudging, energizing. Socrates had several sources of guidance on which to rely, guides well chosen for the long search.

We remember that Socrates had his own *daimones* who warned him when his intended actions were incompatible with the firm precepts of his "sense of I." Maintaining a firm sense of I, an invariable core, demands constant awareness. If consistent honesty, truth, and clarity are the precepts to be upheld, alertness may be supported enormously by appropriate prods and warnings. Socrates' word for his guides and guards, *daimones*, is, for us, uncomfortably close to the word "demon." "Ye watchers and ye holy ones" have also been elicited as such guides. The pitfall of such private communication is, of course, moralism—that superior feeling. And nothing is less apt to be conducive to persuasion than such a stance if it takes over the approach of would-be teachers.

Nevertheless, as a teacher, Socrates knew well that persuasion gives life, brings about change, new direction, and impetus to further learning. All mere amassing of facts is heavy and stultifying. As a true teacher-midwife, Socrates needed Peitho, but he did not call on her directly. Perhaps one of her roles in fifth-century Athens deterred him.

In that remarkable era, Peitho's presence and skillful arbitration were essential to the processes of democratic government. Legal issues were resolved by reasoned debate under her auspices. Such debate must be open to all in the polis, and Athens, as one might expect, set up appropriate public arenas for deliberation, since the citizens were involved in planning what laws and rules they would live under. *Demos*, "the common people," means all citizens. Peitho was actually the civic goddess of democracy, and of *logos*, reasoned speech. She facilitated equal treatment under the law, equal right to speak in assembly, and full political equality. Personal freedom of speech was described with the word *eleutherostomos*, which translated literally means "with a free mouth." The great Greek speakers and politicians knew well that this freedom, if not under the aegis of Peitho, could be used for evil and was a useless freedom unless she guided the selection, expression, and organization of words. Words wound as aptly as they heal; they antagonize as readily as they elicit free and open discussion. Words are potentially as powerful as swords and as soothing as "balm in Gilead." But without words, political freedom is not viable in a democracy. There is little equality in an assembly where individuals cannot express themselves freely and be listened to with attention.

A polis must also have leaders who, with Peitho's help, move the citizens toward the solution of governmental problems. When such leaders advance a potential solution, it must not be defended with a force that could be understood as doing violence to any segment of the citizenry. True leaders are composed, grounded, and centered. Without any evidence of tension, they remain consistently aware of the status and capacities of those they are trying to lead. Staunchly courageous, they defend their allegiance to the values of the polis as well as to their own integrity. Heated debate need not be fueled by anger or disdain; losers feel less defeated when offered respect. These are the attributes of all the most successful leaders in war or peace. They are, of course, also the supreme skills of Ares. Peitho, his daughter, may have learned from him how to be resilient, strong, and responsive to the needs of the polis and to the many who called on her for support and council. In her own creative form of leadership, Peitho did not play the star role but persistently whispered her wise advice to those whose ears were open and tuned to her council.

Such masterly leadership is rare. Luckily, numerous strong and persuasive speeches of fine leaders have been recorded and preserved to illustrate what great statesmen this civilization produced. Socrates, it seems, had no aspirations to be a leader of the polis. Instead of trying to influence a massive audience of assembled Athenians, he focused his skills on guiding young, potential leaders. Socrates actually did value governance by skillful leadership, but the rule he promoted excluded "the people." He believed that governing should be done by "one who knows how" to rule, not by the masses. Socrates was also intolerant of what he considered the poor ability and comprehension of the hoi polloi; he mistrusted their decision-making and governing skills. He was disdainful of the democratic code which provided equal voice and voting power to all citizens of the polis. In these respects, Socrates' ears were not open to Peitho's guidance.

Whether invoked by Socrates or not, Peitho surely

had her eye on him—his art epitomized the strategies of persuasion. Peitho guided Socrates in teaching and arguing in the Socratic way, in discussing and persuading with clarity of purpose and honesty. Under her aegis, Socrates' sharp skills of logical reasoning led to the utter persuasion of truth. Probably she also warned him against the hubris he inevitably revealed when he claimed the special guidance of his private *daimones*. True wisdom, Sophia would concede, is to consistently listen to and follow Peitho in all discourse and relationships.

These, then, were Socrates' guides: Peitho—genuine, honest, grace-filled persuasion—helped him to mellow his abrasive approach to debate and discussion with the magic of tone and well-chosen words; his *daimones*—those protectors of his existential identity—led him toward simplicity, excellence, and integrity; and Sophia—to whom he dedicated his love and his life—drew him into the philosophic way and the search for truth and wisdom.

We have noted that Socrates wrote nothing. Did he believe that for a teacher the spoken word was more vital and persuasive than the written one? Or does this stance of Socrates refer us back to the sages who urged that only the memorized word, learned by ear and spoken from the heart, was truly alive with immediacy and feeling—with persuasion? Even now, we read the prepared statements of politicians with limited interest. Aren't we more persuaded when they speak freely in debate? Some great teachers and political leaders can do both, but only in encounters where minds are open and questions are encouraged and honored. A long presentation, such as the one offered at the symposium, was thought-through, organized, and memorized. Socrates' own head served as computer—he needed to concentrate and record "right now" for future reference. If Socrates never wrote anything it surely was because he believed so firmly in the power, the potency, of verbal communication and its place as a binding force in a community. There was never even a recommended reading list for his students!

Were there others in Athens in Socrates' day with such retentive memories? The great tragic dramas demanded a capacity for memorizing, and able leaders spoke freely and splendidly in the forum. At the height of Athens' greatness, minds were well trained to retain what was learned and observed. Xenophon was one of these remarkable recorders of his times. A fellow Athenian, perhaps ten years older than Plato, he is a rich source of information about Socrates, whom he obviously admired. On reading his reports and comments on Socrates, we sense that Xenophon was no philosopher or student, but rather a perceptive biographer. He was also a historian who recorded in sharp detail the military engagements in which he himself played a leading role. He was an active participant in all facets of Athenian life, which he described with appreciation and took part in with relish. Although he genuinely admired Socrates, he did so without indicating any desire to emulate his way of life or to pursue philosophy as either student or teacher.

Among his copious writings are four books of *Memoirs of Socrates* and *The Banquet*, works which are a testimony to Xenophon's respect for Socrates. A brief look at *The Banquet* will serve as a contrast to Plato's *Symposium*, which we have already considered, and allow us to view Socrates in a more public setting. The banquet takes place in Piraeum, where Callias is gathering a group to celebrate young Autolicus' recent victory in the Olympics. On the way to his home, Callias meets Socrates and other friends, who are then drawn into the group. They bathe and are festively fed and entertained by a buffoon and later by a flute girl, a young dancer, and a beautiful little boy who plays the guitar. This larger gathering is less intimate and orderly than the one depicted in the *Symposium*, yet Xenophon manages to note, in great detail, both conversation and action. Incidently, one guest even prides himself on his ability to recite the *Iliad* and the *Odyssey* by heart—the other guests are not impressed.

The agenda for the long evening of discourse is that each guest, in turn, shall tell what it is "he values himself most upon." Many attributes are mentioned and defended, including beauty, riches, and poverty. Since Socrates is our focus here, we should allow his contribution to reveal what it may of his personality. His statement understandably shocks the whole assembly. He says quite bluntly that his outstanding attribute is "procuring"—to act as a procurer or pimp. He explains this statement by describing his method of getting individuals together who can profit by their mutual acquaintance and perhaps friendship. This linking of individuals who may benefit from sharing their interests implements both social and political interaction in the polis. The group does finally concede, perhaps with some relief, that this is a high-minded and worthy activity.

Later, Critobulus speaks so exuberantly about the importance of his own beauty—even adding the claim that he could easily persuade the dancing girl to kiss him, which not even Socrates could accomplish—that Socrates can't resist interrupting him, saying, "Why, Critobulus, do you give yourself this air of vanity . . . as if you were handsomer than me"?[8] Obviously Socrates is called upon to defend this statement, and an amazing and lively dialogue, which must have delighted the gathering, follows. Offered here is a necessarily abbreviated version:

SOCRATES
Do you believe beauty is no where to be found but in man?

CRITOBULUS
Yes certainly, in other creatures, too, whether animate, as a horse or bull, or inanimate things, as we say that is a handsome sword, or a fine shield, etc.

SOCRATES
But how comes it then, that things so very different as these, should yet all of them be handsome?

CRITOBULUS
Because they are well made, either by art or nature, for the purposes they are employed in.

SOCRATES
Do you know the use of eyes?

CRITOBULUS
To see.

SOCRATES
Well! It is for that very reason mine are handsomer than yours.

CRITOBULUS
Your reason?[9]

Socrates claims that Critobulus' eyes can only see in one direct line, whereas his can see in all directions since they are on a ridge on his face and stare out. Critobulus retorts that at that rate crabs have an advantage over all other eyes. They proceed to discuss noses. Critobulus' nostrils are turned downward, whereas Socrates' are wide and turned up to receive smells from all directions. Also, his nose never hinders sight as does the high nose of Critobulus. Critobulus agrees that Socrates' mouth is bigger, but Socrates goes on to claim that his kisses are more luscious and sweet since his lips are thick and large. Finally, Critobulus says it's impossible to debate with Socrates and calls for a vote from the gathering, who unanimously vote for Critobulus. But Socrates has the last word: "Indeed, Critobulus, your money . . . is able to corrupt a judge upon the bench."[10] This exchange is a fascinating example of how Socrates was able to compensate for the physical defect of his ugliness with sharpness and wit. He had not, in the end, persuaded his audience, but had courageously and successfully defended his self-image. In other words, he had "saved face."

A dispute follows, and people begin speaking together noisily, whereupon Socrates suddenly says that if they are all going to talk at once, they might as well sing together. Ingeniously, he himself initiates this masterful and playful solution. Socrates the "procurer" is capable of filling the role of creative facilitator for the group.

In *Memoirs of Socrates*, Xenophon sums up his appraisal of Socrates' legacy. He states that Socrates "sent no one ever away from him without making him, if willing, a wiser and a happier man. . . . I am persuaded the benefit arising to all those who accompanied with Socrates was not less owing to the irresistible force of his example than to the excellency of his discourses. . . ."[11] That virtue is taught by example, as much as or more than by words, would surely be one of Socrates' basic precepts.

In recent years, Socrates' claim to fame has been challenged. There are those engaged in the political affairs of a modern democracy for whom it is not enough to think and express ideas clearly. Such introspection must, they say, lead to action in which one plays an essential role. This, as we saw earlier, Socrates failed to do. Probably Socrates would justify his withdrawal from political confrontations by pointing to the hazards of involvement in political power struggles. For perspective, the philosopher must withdraw from the combat area and the contest for status and dominance. Obviously, different individuals have, by their very human nature, particular skills and strengths. In formal public debate, where a large audience is to be confronted, Socrates' method of slowly and meticulously revealing a truth was impossible. A large group would be restive, frustrated, and probably angry. Socrates would be at his worst, scornfully defensive. Socrates, one might well believe, disdained anything resembling oratory altogether.

It is also pointed out that Socrates used exceptionally abrasive language when referring to the hoi polloi. They were stupid, uneducated, and unfit to make political decisions, he contended. Plato agreed with him but refrained from using the offensive language to which Socrates resorted. No doubt both were arrogant. As if we, in our enlightened world over two millenia later, never use such derogatory words for any group! Perhaps we just cannily avoid using such language in print. We have even found it necessary to pass defamation laws, though it is costly to go to court. The Greeks were never one hundred percent democratic—women raised their voices only at home, aliens had no vote, and the Greeks were slaveholders. We have, in over two thousand years, made some progress toward democracy, but there is a long way still to go. How can we afford to throw stones backward?

It is risky for us to become too pedantic—too ready to demythologize our heroic models. If we do, we do so at our own loss. Without our legendary mentors, all rebels in one way or another, we would be less resilient and ready to break out of the stultifying mold of binding social conformities. We need these models to help us understand ourselves. Do myths and legends endure that do not in some way deal with our innermost conflicts and unresolved apprehensions—the problems of being human, of living with others in community? Myths and legends offer us a gamut of imagined, vicarious experience. Without this rich legacy we would be impoverished, less empathic, and unrefreshed by the humor of paradox. We must salvage and, with reverence, restore to valid veneration what we can.

We are fortunate to have inherited some historical evidence about the trial of Socrates; from this information we may infer other possibilities to augment our understanding of the political and social climate leading to Socrates' indictment. Trying to fathom why the Athenians decided to prosecute Socrates provides some insight into how communities attempt to defend their boundaries as political entities. How does the individual misfit become quite suddenly so conspicuous in the crowd that has, up to that point, assimilated him? Does such rejection suggest a change in the mood of the crowd, a lack of security and confidence in its own values? After all, the Athenians had tolerated Socrates' idiosyncrasies for seventy years, in which time he had openly talked about his ideas to small groups in the public square and at the baths. He practiced his skills on anyone who felt it wise and safe to take him on in discussion or debate. Each such encounter verified his expertise and consistent stance.

When he was seventy, three citizens accused him of subversive behavior. They claimed that he introduced innovations into the state-supported religious beliefs, confused people as to the nature of good and evil, true and false, and therefore shook the foundations of the state—the polis. They claimed he subverted the young with his talk, that he was antidemocratic, and that, when faced with such charges, he adamantly refused to change his ways. This is the very stuff of legends: the foundation shakers, bold and indomitable; the young, incited; the nervous burghers consolidating and tending toward paranoia. What were the historical factors that played into the uneasy stance of Athenians in the year 399 B.C.? Was it the fresh memory of the devastating rule of the thirty tyrants in 404 B.C. which shook their sense of security in their democratic rule and which perhaps still threatened?

There were three accusers. Had Socrates personally offended one, who then persuaded the other two to join his claim? Why were they so angry, and what made them feel that they could hope for a conviction? Or is it possible that by prosecuting Socrates, they were searching for their own place in history? Their involvement in this trial is their only claim to fame. There have been other such villains. Pontius Pilate would surely never have become a household name were it not for his involvement in another trial.

According to Plato's *Apology*, Meletus, noted only as a not very outstanding poet, was the chosen spokesman of the three. Certainly there must have been a sedately conservative intellectual set in Athens that he may have represented. No doubt the privileged young in Socrates' group tended to be arrogant and had indeed been offensive to such elements of the establishment. A second accuser was Lycon, an orator and intellectual politician, who was definitely a potential target for Socrates' sharp wit and incisive tongue. Orators like Lycon hired the sophists to teach them their skills, but Socrates scoffed at them mercilessly and was not for hire.

Anytus, a rich successful tanner, an outspoken democrat and pillar of tradition, was the most influential of the three accusers. Why was he so infuriated at the son of a stonecutter who lived parsimoniously on a small inherited income? To be a successful tanner required years of hard, smelly, dirty work which must have been strenuous and tiring. He was a loyal citizen and democrat, an advocate of the state religion who took part in political affairs in appropriate fashion. He supported his family and had no time to spend conversing with the rich, pampered young sons of the noble families.

Socrates did none of those things Anytus and many of his fellow citizens and friends considered laudable. He didn't "work" at anything and lived on what his complaining wife seemed to feel was a pittance. As mentioned earlier, he claimed to have superior connections with the gods, who spoke to him through his daimones, thus raising him above others, making him critical and perhaps patronizing. From a working-class background, he nevertheless had pretensions to the prestige of nobility and endowed wealth.

Aside from these points, it is more than probable that Anytus and his family had suffered under the regimes of Critias and Alcibiades, tyrants who had, indeed, been members of the Socratic group. An embittered citizen, Anytus had every reason to be concerned about ancient tradition and its stability. It was true that the epoch of the old truths was slipping away to make room for wider truths in an expanding world. Anxiety and an upsurge of suspicion were shaking old foundations. Such shifts have demanded martyrs.

The pervasiveness of the dis-ease at the trial is indicated by the closeness of the vote. The charges have been made. Socrates has spoken at length in his own defense. The vote of the five hundred jurors is called for and counted—280 against 220—a mere thirty votes would have ensured his acquittal. The verdict is guilty, and Socrates is given a second opportunity to speak before being led away for imprisonment. He himself claims in his final speech that with more time he might have persuaded them of his innocence. Socrates was not actually accused of breaking any law. In fact, no specific evidence of sacrilegious actions or overt attempts at conspiracy is ever introduced in the trial. But Socrates had, evidently for years, been spoiling for a good fight and is defiant to the end. He doesn't, even at the critical moment of defending himself, stoop to lean on the democratic code, to which he had claim.

Throughout his trial, and in his final remarks to the jurors who supported him, Socrates claims vigorously that he does not consider death an evil. In fact, there is much to be said for it, since it seems comparable to a long and dreamless sleep. But if it should be true that it offers a "journey to another place" and that "there are all who have died, what good could be greater?" He lists the legendary ones "who were just in their lives": "What would [one] not give to converse with Orpheus and Musaeus and Hesiod and Homer? I am willing to die many times, if this be true."[12] Socrates invokes the great recorders of myths, those who first gave form in written word, in music and art, to what was then passed along as the most ancient history of a people.

The sentence is to be carried out on the following day in the evening. The whole trial has taken only one day.

The actual drinking of the hemlock, however, is delayed. A truce makes it impossible to carry out the conviction. According to ancient custom, the state ship sailed to Delos every year to commemorate Theseus' rescue of the Minotaur's victims. The ship has not yet returned to Athens; no condemned person could be put to death before its arrival. An epic character, Socrates uses every moment of this delay to drive home his message into the hearts and memories of his followers, rather than save himself.

During the many days of discussion with his followers, while in prison, Socrates insists that the thrust of their deliberations should be an effort to set aside judgment on what happened at the trial. Human nature must be understood and not discussed judgmentally. The majority of people are neither good nor bad, and this holds for their thought and speech as well as for their actions. However, one's reasoning must be sound even though "we ourselves are not yet sound." For such soundness one must consistently strive.[13]

It is our good fortune, as well as that of his devoted students, that the winds allowed for these long final days. But the winds finally do change and the ship does arrive from Delos. What a dramatic marvel the last long hours become. Socrates plays his role brilliantly throughout the discussions that lead to the consummation of his own legend. Before a final meeting with his young companions, Socrates has a private discussion with his old friend, Crito. They have been close for many years, and Crito has come to the prison early in the morning to be alone with Socrates in order to try to persuade him to run away. It can still be managed rather easily—everything is organized—but this is, indeed, the eleventh hour.

Socrates defends his determination to go through with the sentence even though Crito claims it was an unjust one. Crito also reminds Socrates that the vote was close and that he lost by only thirty votes out of the total five hundred cast by the jurors. Socrates, however, is not moved. He claims that he is under a contractual obligation to the laws of the commonwealth where he has been a citizen all his life. Where should he escape to with wife and children? he asks. No other city compares with Athens, the city that has supported and sustained him for seventy years. And he would never have agreed to change his way of living and teaching if the jurors accepted such a pledge as a basis for acquittal. In fact, he had defended himself, and his way of being, forcefully at the trial: ". . . as long as I have breath and strength I will not cease from philosophy, and from exhorting you, and declaring the truth to every one of you whom I meet. . . ." He even faced his jurors with a direct challenge: ". . . either acquit me, or do not acquit me: but be sure that I shall not alter my way of life; no, not if I have to die for it many times."[14]

Socrates the man and his way of life are of one piece, fused in the very core of his being. Losing his way of life would be death itself. This does not, however, make for a social, adaptable identity. Such a man is truly a thorn in the social body, a gadfly in a complacent political order, in a polis. Such a man is also extremely rare. There is something super-human and unnerving about his firm stance. The fervency of a religious faith is expressed with unremitting integrity. We are awed by Socrates' immutable conviction and resonate to its challenge. The Athenians were right—he did not "believe" in their gods. He neither attacked their customs nor belittled their relationships to the Olympian hierarchy, but he did have a private belief system, with the direct voices of his daimones to guide him. In late-twentieth-century words, I believe Socrates was claiming that the soul is the invariable core of man or woman. It has been called, in life cycle terms, the innermost sense of I—the "I am" of a person—the individual existential identity, not to be confused with the psychosocial identity which adapts, more or less, to the social norms of the milieu.

On the final morning when the young men arrive at the prison, they are instructed to wait, because the officials are removing Socrates' fetters to allow him freedom, a final day of movement. His wife, Xanthippe, and his infant son are there but are sent away, she "weeping bitterly and beating her breast." "Crito, let her be taken home," says Socrates.[15] This last day of dialogue with his students begins, then, with Socrates sitting up on his bed, rubbing his legs with pleasure in the sensation of their release from the accustomed bindings. The young, handsome men are clustered around him, curious, eager not to miss a word, a look, or a gesture. And Phaedo, the recorder of the legendary last day of Socrates, is there close by the bed, his stylus poised, his quill ready.

He is serious, troubled, his head bent industriously over his work. Perhaps Phaedo has been alerted by Plato, who usually played the role of dedicated student and recorder, not to miss a single word or intonation. Indeed, the concentration of topics and ideas and the discussion of each item add up to a long, circuitous account. But why is Plato not present? There is a claim of illness. One may well believe that his worried family urged a trip on their son after Socrates' trial. He must have seemed to them very much at risk in a nervous Athens so bent on conformity.

Phaedo describes a personally meaningful memory which depicts the intimacy of the scene:

> I will tell you. I was sitting by the bed on a stool at his right hand, and his seat was a good deal higher than mine. He stroked my head and gathered up the hair on my neck in his hand—you know he used often to play with my hair—and said, To-morrow, Phaedo, I daresay you will cut off these beautiful locks.
>
> I suppose so, Socrates, I replied.
>
> You will not, if you take my advice.
>
> Why not? I asked.
>
> You and I will cut off our hair today, he said, if our argument be dead indeed, and we cannot bring it to life again. . . .[16]

Cutting one's hair was apparently a common way of expressing grief in Greece. Women tore their hair and scratched their faces, in this manner "defacing" themselves as a demonstration of their grief. Greek depictions of the figures of men show long and, even more frequently, curly hair. Phaedo obviously had such hair. Beards and curls were evidence of virility as well as beauty and health. In any case, what had been an intimate and possibly emotional exchange between Phaedo and Socrates is transformed into an intellectual challenge. How Socratic!

We are eager to hear verbatim from Phaedo what loomed on this last day as topics of major importance. Phaedo writes:

> But Socrates sat up on the bed, and bent his leg and rubbed it with his hand, and while he was rubbing it said to us, How strange a thing is what men call pleasure! How wonderful is its relation to pain, which seems to be the opposite of it! They will not come to a man together: but if he pursues the one and gains it, he is almost forced to take the other also, as if they were two distinct things united at one end.[17]

This sensory and very ordinary action of rubbing his legs offers a tangible example of the philosophic truth which Socrates then pursues. A physical touch has set off the inevitable topic of the day—the relation of the opposites, birth and death linked together by life. A universal experience has rather playfully dramatized a philosophic concept and the conversation is under way:

> Indeed, as I am setting out on a journey to the other world, what could be more fitting for me than to talk about my journey, and to consider what we imagine to be its nature? How could we better employ the interval between this and sunset?[18]

Since Socrates had consistently refused all efforts to help him escape, one other immediate—and still debated—topic needed to be considered: Does a man have the right to take his own life by his own hand? This question is first discussed and then set aside by Socrates with the claim that man "must wait until God sends some necessity upon him as has now been sent to me."[19] Is the command of a strong inner voice, which may demand life itself, intrinsic to the call of the legendary figure?

Socrates is confident that the dead have an existence after life and that this new life is far better for the good than for the wicked. He relates a statement of Orphic doctrine, with which he is evidently well acquainted, about the souls of the dead:

> There is an ancient belief, which we remember, that on leaving this world they exist there, and that they return hither and are born again from the dead. But if it be true that the living are born from the dead, our souls must exist in the other world: otherwise they could not be born again.[20]

Socrates feels impelled to ground this point on a wider, more general base. He states, "Let us consider whether or no the souls of men exist in the next world after death."[21] The answer must be proved in relation to all things that are "generated"—in other words, is everything generated from its opposite? A long listing of opposites leads to the relation of sleeping to waking, and from there to life's relation to death. If life generates death, what does its opposite, death, generate? Of course, a return to life. So, "the souls of the dead must exist somewhere, whence they come into being again."[22] The group similarly determines that the soul must be immortal. We may well wonder how a man facing death, yet still so keenly alive, could bring himself and those with him to coolly discuss exactly what prospect the innermost soul has of finding a return to life after death.

The group also considers the doctrine of *anamnesis*, or recall, which holds that our learning is only a process of recollection of something previously known in a former life. Lapse of time causes forgetfulness of our past learning and experience. Recollection takes place only if questions are asked "in the right way"—the great art of the true philosopher. This "right way" stirs something deep in the mind, an experience of valid knowledge particular to oneself. Does *anamnesis* convincingly prove that the soul remains intact after death, since this former knowledge is preserved? The group wonders, and the question arises whether after death the soul can avoid being scattered "to the winds of death." Socrates offers to discuss this question, and a new lightness of tone enters the dialogue.

Like children, you are afraid that the wind will really blow the soul away and disperse her when she leaves the body; especially if a man happens to die in a storm and not in a calm.

Cebes laughed and said, Try and convince us as if we were afraid, Socrates; or rather, do not think that we are afraid ourselves. Perhaps there is a child within us who has these fears. Let us try and persuade him not to be afraid of death, as if it were a bugbear.

You must charm him every day, until you have charmed him away, said Socrates.[23]

These remarks are delightful, and particularly so since "the child within" is so seldom given attention or credence in philosophic discourse. Since the foundation of our whole inner world rests on the understanding developed in early childhood experience, it is a basic flaw to disregard its importance. Moreover, with trust and hope, good and bad, just and unjust, and the wonder of beauty all so directly and deeply experienced in early years, how could this vital early learning be so casually valued by Socrates and his students? Their idea of reincarnation as the main source of our enduring attitudes and recollections seems like an un-socratic leap of logic. These would-be philosophers do, however, recognize and remember fear as a component of childhood experience; boys were obviously meant to "measure up" and be brave. Under the guidance of gods who had themselves known no childhood—did not gradually mature and change—childhood and its rich resources could apparently be ignored. At least Socrates was persuaded that "wonder," that priceless gift of childhood, was of value: One day, on meeting Theaetatus, a bright young boy, Socrates remarked that he felt sure Theaetatus had thought a great deal. The youngster answered, "Not that, but I have wondered a great deal." Socrates replied, "Ah, that shows the lover of wisdom . . . for wisdom begins in wonder."[24]

The considerations preoccupying the group become more general, and topics such as the relation of the Idea to all sides of human reality are reviewed: the Beautiful, that perfection which reveals itself in form; the Good in its power; and Truth with its religious element, the grail object of the philosophic quest; all infused the passionate search for knowledge which was Greek and of that remarkable century. This indefatigable group of devoted scholars considers at length what is destructible—what the senses provide information about; and what is indestructible—the soul and its involvement with the invisible, with ideas and pure knowledge. Since the soul will remain intact and will proceed after death to a place where it will dwell with the good and the wise, the group decides that one must prepare throughout life for this future by lovingly pursuing wisdom, by concentrating on philosophy, which will set the soul free.

In contrast to this philosophic way, the Orphic way, we will recall, includes purity and care for the body as well as for the soul. The philosophic way demands little concern for the corporeal health, purity, and well-being of the philosopher, for whom the mind and the soul are the foci of interest. The Orphic way accepts a relationship between the mind and the body and incorporates both in the mysteries. Socrates, unlike most philosophers, may have acknowledged this, for he took pride in his physical well-being.

The long, convoluted discourse of the day, in which each argument is first selected and weighed as worthy of recognition and then every question meticulously answered, seems endless. The concentration of the group has been phenomenal. And the teacher, who, we remind ourselves, is seventy years old and sitting on his deathbed, has amazed us in his vigorous pursuit of the vital topics discussed. Socrates, perhaps becoming aware of the fading light of this long last day, then very movingly and with deep caring states:

> I shall not be anxious to persuade my audience that I am right, except by the way; but I shall be very anxious indeed to persuade myself. For see, my dear friend, how selfish my reasoning is. If what I say is true, it is well to believe it. But if there is nothing after death, at any rate I shall pain my friends less by my lamentations in the interval before I die.[25]

He goes on to say, with unsimulated humility, that they must oppose him with every argument they have, so that "in my anxiety to convince you, I do not deceive both you and myself, and go away, leaving my sting behind me, like a bee."[26]

Any possible hidden agendas that could lurk behind his argument are dealt with one by one and forthrightly in this passage:

> "I shall not be anxious to persuade my audience that I am right"—I concede that I may be wrong.

> "I shall be very anxious indeed to persuade myself"— My *own* mind is still wide open.

> "For see, my dear friend, how selfish my reasoning is"—I expose my own bias freely.

> "If what I say is true, it is well to believe it"—Your minds should always be open to truth.

> "But if there is nothing after death, at any rate I shall pain my friends less by my lamentations in the interval

before I die"—I obviously wish to cause you, my friends, less pain by my argument—another bias.

". . . and go away, leaving my sting behind me, like a bee"—leaving my invalidating biases and distortions behind me.

There is no clearer invocation of Peitho in this whole persuasive discourse. Open-minded, honest, free interchange is the goal of discussion, presentation, and debate. The evidence presented is, as far as it is known and understood, the only firm foundation that exists. Personal biases are revealed. No secret agendas, which insidiously poison the relationships of discussants with one another, intrude in the dialogue. A mutual, earnest search for the truth is under way. Here is Socrates at his greatest—Peitho whispering in his ear and no doubt his *daimones* standing by firmly.

To achieve such unadulterated interchange seems, of course, impossibly utopian, nonhuman. Humans, being anxious and torn, can only tenaciously strive, honor the striving, and preserve the legacy of true mentors, those who have stood fast. Pure truth—objectivity—is beyond us, but we can strive toward a disciplined subjectivity.

Socrates gives his pupils a final instruction:

If it be true, that the soul is immortal, we have to take care of her, not merely on account of the time which we call life, but also on account of all time.[27]

This commitment, he maintains, is the way of the philosopher.

What was the tone of Socrates' voice on this last

absorbing day—crisp, strident, low, high? He scorned oratory! On that day, one would like to think that he spoke warmly as he declared his devotion to Sophia, the Lady Wisdom. It is important that we feel this warmth, for otherwise the legend would be less moving and powerful.

The closing scene, in its simplicity, is utterly dramatic; Socrates makes it so straightforward, in fact, his words and actions are direct and practical. As the daylight fades, he tries to set a matter-of-fact, no-nonsense tone which includes some genuine consideration for the workers of the world:

> . . . it is time for me to betake myself to the bath. I think that I had better bathe before I drink the poison, and not give the women the trouble of washing my dead body.[28]

It was only for sham, in all its aspects, that he had contempt.

On Socrates' return to the awaiting group, Crito asks him for final directions about care for his family and for themselves. "How shall we serve you best?" Socrates' answer is: "Simply by doing what I always tell you, Crito. Take care of your own selves, and you will serve me and mine and yourselves in all that you do. . . ."[29]

When the poison is presented to him he drinks it calmly.

Does a man die whose memory lives on for centuries in legend and in our hearts and aspirations? Perhaps his appeal to us, human as we are, is just because he could be cantankerous like the rest of us, as well as wise and lovable. When he became too contentious, Peitho undoubtedly gave him a nudge.

At least one portrait of Socrates exists: the painting *Death of Socrates,* by the French artist Jacques Louis David, dated approximately 1800, depicts his drinking of the lethal hemlock, while surrounded by mourning students and companions. Here we see him as an aristocratic figure making a gracious, inclusive gesture toward his devoted followers.

But how would Socrates wish to be remembered—as the dedicated Athenian teacher coolly discussing philosophical matters on his deathbed? Or should we, perhaps, recast him as the goatlike Marsyas; or even as Silenus, the buffoonish companion of Dionysus, who, though usually riding on an ass, is nonetheless filled with precious gold?

What an achievement for Socrates, the ugly one, to successfully defy the prevailing assumption that ugly is bad, that the physically beautiful is necessarily good, and, by his transcendence of his misfortune, to win for himself an immortality centuries have acknowledged. In Socrates' own, idiosyncratic way, he carved his own image—chiseled out of firm Greek rock, like the lovely columns that have endured through the centuries, upright, full of grace, aspiring, but firmly earthbound.

Clearly Socrates loved life, loved people, nature, his city, and was not unwilling to express this joy in song, dance, and sociability—what a wonderful life. Perhaps what might please him most would be to know that more than two thousand years after his death we are trying to put him together out of pieces like those in a puzzle. That, I believe, would delight him. Maybe the outlandish costume of the jester, with its bells and bright piebald colors, or the

Death of Socrates.

exaggerated makeup of the clown, is the appropriate disguise of the truly wise man, the wise man-jester for all seasons.

So let us drink our own final hemlock in celebration of the wise fools who learn to laugh at adversity, transcending lack and loss with integrity, compassion, and humor.

Epilogue

Hesiod, who appears in the preliterate era of Greek history as a historian with foreknowledge of the future, paints a dark picture of the development of civilization. The prophecy is grim, outdoing Cassandra in its foreboding. In his *Works and Days*, Hesiod outlines five ages of man. In the first, a generous earth provides fruits in abundance with no need for human toil and burdensome defense. This is the Golden Age—a race of mortals ruled by Cronus. Life is good, death swift and painless—"they died as though subdued by sleep." In time, however, Pandora, "a beautiful evil," is introduced, and with her come strife and disease.

The Silver Age follows. Mankind is selfish and immature; there is recklessness, hubris, and disrespect for the gods. Then the Bronze Age emerges. Men venerate Ares, god of war; they are huge, strong, and full of hubris, and go down to Hades namelessly. The Heroic Age takes over next. Old age is never achieved because men kill one another off in famous wars. Finally comes the Iron Age. Grief and apprehension rule night and day. Wretchedness is everywhere. The old are neglected and abandoned; there is no time or room for real maturity, for allowing a ripening to old age.

How telling that history could be mapped out and progress defined in terms of the development of a metallurgy that utilizes progressively baser materials with increasingly lethal potential—metals which expand the power of men to defend themselves more readily and to attack more powerfully. Hesiod foretold ominous, trouble-filled times. Unfortunately he offered no solutions to guide his country, its neighbors, and future cultures in how to avoid such developments. The twentieth century has been beset with such times. Today, metallurgy has turned to steel and other alloys. Is it now the Steel Age? "Steel" we could call it, exulting in our brilliant technology. "Steal" we must spell it when we consider our insatiable greed, our despoliation of the planet Earth with resulting pollution and depletion, and our exploitation of neighboring peoples whenever it has been possible and profitable.

At home, in our own communities, all exits and entrances are under lock and key—plus alarm systems. Greed prevails; the locksmiths flourish. Abroad our country exploits for economic profit and employs violent, imperialistic tactics in its enthusiasm for democracy and its desire to expand its sphere of power. One method has been to denigrate others, to make them a pseudo-species or "barbarians," as the Greeks had it, in order to justify the intention to dominate or eliminate them. Splendid technical weapons, produced at enormous cost, allow us to demand our form of rule even in distant countries. The cost of this self-righteous stance leaves our own children, elders, and the sick uncared for and many families homeless. Why try to rule the world at all? As yet we have not learned to rule ourselves.

In *Works and Days*, Hesiod was, of course, interested only in describing the development of a man's world. Women may indeed and probably did have influence, but their power was blatantly nil. Such suppression of all things female was apparently used to free men and their hubris from the timelessly old and previously prevailing rule of the mother—the earth goddesses. Today, mortals have completely abandoned the earth goddesses and ruthlessly despoil, rob, and poison the earth. Only basic change from this course can prevent the globe from becoming moon dust.

How many of us have not despaired at the way in which history repeats itself, how violence, war, raises its ugly head again and again. How difficult it is for us to change—to assess, to plan, and to implement the changes necessary for our planet to endure. Human beings do have the capacity for change, but our pace is snail-like in contrast to the speed of degradation in our environment, our habitat. Only a massive, concerted effort can save this planet. Cooperation and interdependence on a worldwide scale are obviously mandatory for survival.

One strong source of hope is developing. We are learning to speak not only with those who speak our own language but with all the other peoples of the world. It is vital that this exchange be vigorously pursued. We must learn, translate, travel, and come to know and accept the fact that we are all one species. Technology now makes this communication possible. Words can be conveyed faster than flight.

Satellite images make world events immediate and visibly present; machines can convey human bodies anywhere there is a safe landing. And energy *is* available, the immeasurable energy of the sun, the planets, the earth itself and its plenitude of resources. With expert care, this energy can be tapped without disrupting the balanced interdependence of the natural forces. Technology can dehumanize us, but can also be a means toward understanding one another. With determination and cooperation we may eventually reroute its uses into saner, less destructive channels.

Catastrophe needs to be shared and alleviated. Trouble, violence, or disaster in any place on earth is cause for universal concern and should be a mandate for non-violent, cooperative action. The price of neglect is too high. Isolation is no longer possible—what affects one sector touches all. Neither is there, perhaps there never was, a place to hide where evil discord can rule in private. Even the power of the family is challenged as we become more aware of how the malaise of society is often powerfully and insidiously manifest in this institution. Political thought has illuminated a distinction between the realms of private and public life which reflects, with remarkable symmetry, the double standard inherent in the way nations conduct their "foreign affairs." In both cases, domestic values do not necessarily apply to neighbors; "family first" has been considered an acceptable creed—followed by the community, the party, the polis. Here in America we have a so-called "melting pot," but are hard pressed to treat all citizens equally. Perhaps we should strive for a mosaic instead of a soup and, in that way, preserve all the nuances of color and culture.

The twentieth century has shocked us with evidence of what horrors and baseness human beings are capable—greed, ruthlessness, and violence. Despair is natural. Yet there are still great men and women who justify our hope that human beings are also capable of change, of generous caring, of valiant striving for justice, truth, and beauty, toward a vision of a global family. Dare we fervently hope to establish the twenty-first century as the Age of Communication and to develop in it a deeper expression of human mutuality? Can we grow beyond our age-old patterns of contempt and pseudo-speciation when our own, often admirable, attachment to community may cause us to exclude outsiders and to see them as enemies, even as nonhuman?

Most earnestly we should enlist Peitho and all of her most salient skills and strengths to help build bridges of language and of art, to cross the distances that distort our understanding of one another. Could we not be persuaded to focus our concerted attention on the rehabilitation of the globe, that lovely, bright Earth our moon-astronauts saw shining gloriously blue-green in the empty, arid void of the cosmos? It was not Asia, Africa, or America they saw but one world, one planet. They hoped, of course, to land on target, but any landing on this verdant globe would, to them, have been home.

So here we are on this orbed planet, though few have been privileged the perspective that astronauts are granted. We do, however, have the recorded legends of the past and the hindsight perspective of history. We can draw out from these sources the heroes, the wise ones, the motivated iconlike figures who light our way and give our lives meaning and courage to bring about constructive change.

This book has dealt with three such figures; it has retold the myths and legends that incorporated their stories and focused on the attributes and strengths of each individual character. In Prometheus we saw the figure of a mythical demigod who, risking the displeasure of a tyrant god, compassionately came to the rescue of endangered mortals. He acted in response to what he felt to be a grave injustice and was severely punished. This penalty—bonds, exposure, and torture—he could have avoided by revealing his secret foreknowledge of the fate awaiting Zeus, but that would have meant disarming himself and giving in to injustice. Relying on his own endurance and his resolution, daily, to resist that temptation, he remains forever an icon of rocklike determination. Such fortitude can inspire energy-filled hope in us. It can activate us, especially those of us *not* bound, in the service of supporting justice against tyranny.

The gifts Prometheus bestowed on humankind—metallurgy, alchemy, technology—are frightening in their capacity for destruction, but are also constructive in their promise of creativity. Was this power safer in the hands of the Olympian gods than with humans? Mortals, luckily, are held back somewhat by shame, doubt, and guilt, which are capable of checking our overriding impulsiveness. And, unlike the gods, who can control events anywhere in the cosmos with the snap of a finger, "creatures of a day" must continually accept the limitations imposed on them by space and time. Under these constraints, humans need to be aroused to action; they depend on hope to "help them cease foreseeing doom." Prometheus, because of his "pity" on humankind, was, therefore, the donor of tremendous gifts—enlightenment, protection, creativity. He also gave us vision and hope that we might learn to use his gifts with compassion and foresight.

Orpheus, who symbolizes creativity in all the arts, supports us in other, not less heroic, ways. We have in him the figure of the mortal who, with courage and the priceless gift of song, undertakes a task involving seemingly insurmountable obstacles. Early in his journey Orpheus succeeds quite miraculously and senses the prospect of complete success. But at the final step, he fails. We, having all experienced both trivial and major failure in our lives and in our work, respond with empathy; he too is mortal, he is one of us. Our reactions to failure, however, are very different from his. We droop, we commiserate, and worst of all we are ashamed and lose heart. Orpheus, on the other hand, makes music of his feelings: he sings his sadness, his sense of loss, his sense of defeat and shame. All nature, all animals, and human beings respond. Of course they respond—he expresses through his music all the wordless pain that life can and does bring day by day and all night long. Ah yes, we say, we understand. We accept the fact that we are not isolated and unique but share daily shame and loss and can do so more resolutely if we face it together.

This acceptance can generate an opening to creative impulse which results in transcendent vitality and a new direction. Orpheus empowers our capacity to see, hear, touch, smell, taste, and move with attentive keen senses; our lives are thus enriched by our perception of the beautiful and by taking part in its creation. What gift could be more healing? No wonder the artists of life and living, the artists of making and doing, have kept Orpheus alive for us all through the centuries.

Unlike Orpheus, Socrates was not a loser; when he did lose, he instigated the loss himself, it was his choice. Rather, his fate was from early on to be the child who lacks, who, in shining Athens, had no physical beauty, in fact was ugly. So did he sulk, feel ashamed, and fail? No, he set himself the task of rising above his deprivation. He was exemplary in his living patterns, studiously simple in his demands, pursuing the active well-being of his body and conforming with the laws of the polis.

He undertook the study and search for wisdom inherent in philosophy. His goal was to unveil the infallibility of truth—the beauty and strength of authenticity which can be found in the invariable core of the human being, the beauty of the "inner man," as he described it. He nurtured these convictions in his followers; he lived these precepts throughout his life. The role he chose to play, and played so well, gave him great freedom. He was able to participate in Athenian life and society without wholly identifying with its values. He remained apart and was therefore able to see and enjoy the foibles, ambitions, and curious identity problems of those with whom he socialized. Of course he was amused, and he teased with his talk, which entertained him as much as his audience. His pursuit of wisdom would have lost its resilience had he not been blessed with playful humor, humor for all occasions, and a responsive joy in life.

He was not perfect, surely not a good husband, probably not a fighting democrat, and who knows what kind of a father. But he was a wonderful teacher and model both for his Athenian students and for us today. He was just a mortal, but what a person! We are beholden to Plato and Xenophon for their verbal portraits.

In these pages we have introduced another, less familiar figure, Peitho, goddess of persuasion, who speaks a language of reconciliation, mutuality, and *agape*. We have traced her propensities, her power in the lives of our legendary figures, but she does not stand out clearly as a personality, a goddess. She appears, usually with Aphrodite or Eros, in a line-drawn, sketchy way on vases and urns. Her deeds have been recorded in Greek myths, and the great playwrights introduced her and reported her interventions in their dramas. But only phrases such as "lovely Peitho," "soft-eyed Peitho," "smooth-voiced Peitho," "charming Peitho," truly give us a sense of her presence. Is it perhaps the nature of her power to remain a subtle, muselike spirit whose approach varies according to the attributes, hearing acuity, and openness of the one into whose ear she is whispering?

When we have tried to portray our most cherished values—justice, hope, and liberty—they have been given form in statuary, as idealized figures of women on pedestals: Justice with her eyes bound; Liberty with a torch; and patient Hope with arms outstretched. Peitho should join these figures: as a means of resolving differences fairly and more permanently,

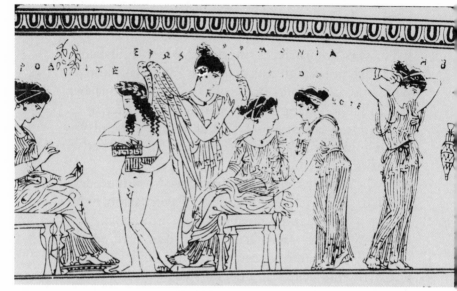

Scene on a wool-carder's knee guard. Peitho (probably the figure holding a mirror) with Aphrodite, Eros, Harmonia, and Kore.

Nemesis, with Tyche, points at Peitho; Aphrodite holds Helen on her lap.

she symbolizes the only alternative to violence. If violence remains a primary method for solving national and international problems, we will always have wars. Honest persuasion is our only valid recourse for settling disputes both at home and abroad.

But these venerated, symbolic figures all could be energized! As abstractions in stone they are adulated, but are impotent and immobile; they are not stirring or touching, and obviously are not moving. What a farce! Why don't living women at last gather their pent-up energies and hum like the chorus in "Prometheus Unbound"? Let the sound be a vibrant HUM of energy—for humus, the earth, for humanity, humor, humility, humane tenderness and compassion. Those have been the breath and tone, the song of womankind. Let the sound ring loud and clear—an organic chord like a rising tide demanding change in our fundamental goals as well as in the small details of the way we live, cherish, and value ourselves, others, and the planet.

Some great thrust of energetic purpose, motivated and supported by genuine hope, could surge us forward into a non-violent, Peitho-led future where wars and rumors of wars would no longer eclipse our need to care for the earth and humankind. But this process will be slow and arduous. We will fail often and be required to tolerate such failures, to make further efforts and realign our relationships. Courage lies in risking failure, in using each temporary loss to promote a more energized movement toward a goal of peaceful interdependence.

We are all guilty—guilty of injustice, bias, hubris, as well as apathy. Individual goals and false hopes block any effort that demands discomfort or deprivation. We have become dependent and weakened by our luxuries. We need to be aroused, literally stirred up by the energy of Heracles, and guided by Peitho to empathic conciliation. In this process we could learn to know and appreciate the positive attributes of those who inhabit this planet, our world community. Even if we are wary of the power and objectives of other nations, we can still be persuaded, by the greatness of their art, that they are noble and that they understand the relationship of truth to beauty and the difference between integrity and small-minded values. If other cultures have maintained an allegiance to nature, its wonders and its nurturance, we should surely bow in respect, for as modern westerners we have clearly failed to preserve this most essential relationship. To those who honor the land and living things, we must seem like barbarians—we took over a rich and glorious new-found land and in so short a time have despoiled it mindlessly. Perhaps Peitho could encourage in us a dollop of humility in our approach to others who suffer from lack of technical know-how but excel in many other aspects of their cultural development.

We need hope, active hope which supports and strengthens if we honor its true nature. We often use the word "hope" carelessly to convey what is actually casual wishful thinking or numerous vaguely floating preferences, whims. In daily usage "hope" has met with the same fate as the word "love"; both words could benefit by a rest and reappraisal. We all have dreams and hopes, but they remain idiosyncratic and varied. The outcome of hoping is dependent on the energy we muster and employ to reach the goal. Hope which does not support and germinate the seeds of action leading to fruition, that leaves necessary responsibility to change, to others, or to the gods, is a cop-out, a travesty. The rocking-chair variety of dreaming and hoping may be pleasant, but is flabby and delusive, the opiate of the well-meaning inactivist.

Correctly used, the word "hope" has a timeless, encompassing quality that can only be compared with the promise and energy incorporated in the seed, all the seeds, that nature extravagantly throws out in a lavish distribution for the continuance of natural life and verdure on our planet. There is hope—generative hope—based on trust in the abounding grace, the northern lights, the music of the spheres, and the word. Hope is our spur; hope is our motivation to muster our creative capacities and focus them on the goal of loving our planet and ensuring its vital survival.

Notes

Prologue

1. Eric Partridge, *Origins: A Short Etymological Dictionary of Modern English* (New York: Macmillan, 1958), p. 424.

2. Plato, *Phaedrus* 279, freely translated by William Alfred.

Prometheus

1. Aeschylus, *Prometheus Bound*, trans. David Grene, in *The Complete Greek Tragedies: Aeschylus II*, eds. David Grene and Richmond Lattimore (New York: Washington Square Press, 1967), pp. 148–49.

2. Ibid., pp. 156–57.

3. Ibid., p. 153.

4. Ibid., p. 174.

5. Ibid., p. 175.

6. See G. Karl Galinsky, *The Herakles Theme* (Oxford, 1972), noted in *Gods and Heroes of the Greeks: The Library of Apollodorus*, trans. and ed. Michael Simpson (Amherst: University of Massachusetts Press, 1976), pp. 108–9, 118.

7. Tomb inscription, trans. Plumptre, in A. E. Haigh, *The Tragic Drama of the Greeks* (Oxford: Clarendon Press, 1906), p. 59.

8. Aeschylus, *Agamemnon*, trans. Richmond Lattimore, in *Greek Tragedies*, Vol. 1, eds. David Grene and Richmond Lattimore (Chicago: Chicago University Press, 1960), p. 12.

9. Aeschylus, *Prometheus Bound*, pp. 148–49.

10. Ibid., pp. 146–47.

11. Ibid., p. 180.

Notes

Orpheus

1. Joanne Greenberg, *Rites of Passage* (New York: Holt, Rinehart & Winston, 1972), p. 184.

2. See W.K.C. Guthrie, *Orpheus and Greek Religion* (New York: Norton, 1966), pp. 28–29.

3. *Argonautica*, 1.1134ff., 4.1409, trans. A. B. Kolenkow, in Walter Burkert, "Orphism and Bacchic Mysteries: New Evidence and Old Problems of Interpretation," Protocol of the twenty-eighth colloquy of the Center for Hermeneutical Studies, March 1977, p. 25.

4. I am indebted to W.K.C. Guthrie, *Orpheus and Greek Religion*, in my review of these texts.

5. Guthrie, op. cit., pp. 120–22, 203.

6. Goldplate from Thessaly, *A Greek Prayer*, in Burkert, op. cit., p. 10.

7. Mircea Eliade, *Shamanism*, Bollingen Series LXXVI (Princeton, N.J.: Princeton University Press, 1972), pp. 508–9.

8. Elizabeth Sewell, *The Orphic Voice: Poetry and Natural History* (New Haven: Yale University Press, 1960).

Socrates

1. Plato, *The Symposium*, trans. Walter Hamilton (London: Penguin, 1951), p. 100.

2. Plato, *Symposium*, pp. 75–79.

3. Ibid., p. 79.

4. Ibid., pp. 79–81.

5. Ibid., pp. 86–90.

6. Erik H. Erikson, *Childhood and Society* (New York: Norton, 1950).

7. Plato, *Symposium*, pp. 108–10.

8. Xenophon, *The Banquet*, trans. J. Welwood, in *The Complete Works of Xenophon* (Edinburgh: William P. Nimmo, 1881), p. 610.

9. Ibid., p. 615.

10. Ibid., p. 616.

11. Xenophon, *Memoirs of Socrates*, trans. Sarah Fielding, in *The Complete Works of Xenophon* (Edinburgh: William P. Nimmo, 1881), p. 529.

12. Plato, *Apology*, trans. Basil Wrighton, in Romano Guardini, *The Death of Socrates* (New York: Meridian, 1962), p. 65.

13. Plato, *Phaedo*, trans. Basil Wrighton, in Guardini, op. cit., p. 140.

14. Plato, *Apology*, pp. 46–47.

15. Plato, *Phaedo*, p. 97.

16. Ibid., p. 138.

17. Ibid., p. 97.

18. Ibid., p. 99.

19. Ibid., p. 100.

20. Ibid., p. 109.

21. Ibid.

22. Ibid., p. 111.

23. Ibid., p. 122.

24. Plato, *Theaetatus*, as translated in Edith Hamilton, *The Greek Way to Western Civilization* (New York: Norton, 1942), p. 90.

25. Plato, *Phaedo*, pp. 140–41.

26. Ibid., p. 141.

27. Ibid., p. 167.

28. Ibid., p. 173.

29. Ibid., p. 174.

Credits

Page 17: Courtesy of the National Archaeological Museum, Athens.

Facing page 20: Spectrum Colour Library, England.

Page 79: Robinson, *Catalog of Boston Vases*, frontis.

Facing page 116: Fine Arts Photographic Library Ltd., London; Edmond Aman-Jean 1860–1935: Orpheus and His Muse. Courtesy of Art Licensing International Inc., New York.

Page 121: Copyright the Trustees of the British Museum.

Page 124: C. M. Dixon Photo Resources, Colour Photo Library, England.

Page 175: The Metropolitan Museum of Art, Wolfe Fund, 1931. Catharine Lorillard Wolfe Collection.

Page 186: Courtesy Cambridge University Press, New York.

Page 186: Courtesy Cambridge University Press, New York.